Creative Giving

Creative Giving

*Understanding Planned Giving
and Endowments in Church*

MICHAEL REEVES,
ROB FAIRLY,
AND SANFORD COON

DISCIPLESHIP RESOURCES

PO BOX 340003 • NASHVILLE, TN 37203-0003
www.discipleshipresources.org

From Rob Fairly

I am grateful for my parents, who instilled in me both an appreciation of life and the love God gives us, as well as the concept that generosity is an expression of that love. Thanks to my wife Pam and my three wonderful children, Jennifer, Susannah, and Tripp, who make that life truly full. Thanks to the staff of the United Methodist Foundation of Louisiana for making the work fun. In particular, I am grateful to the leadership of Michael Reeves, whose passion in life is to make clear the connection between our faith and our money.

From Sanford Coon

In gratitude for the mystery and marvel of generations—fore, aft, and in between: parents Carlos and Dionitia, who modeled the Christian faith and were diligent teachers through its practice; children Mark Kenner and Ellen Ashley, who taught through questions by word and deed the nature of God's love and the power of trust; grandchildren Meagan Andrea, Thomas Marc, Ellen Anne, and one more on the way, who truly are the new generation and so must yet learn the dynamic blessing and oneness of giving and receiving; wife Mary Ellen, who has lovingly taught me the richness of spiritual practice, with whom I made my first planned gift, and who can now reclaim the breakfast table for dining.

From Michael Reeves

I dedicate this work to my children, Jason and Keith, and their children, Avery, James, and Julia, who could be the beneficiaries of creative giving. Thanks to my friends and colleagues Rob Fairly and Sandy Coon for their insights, contributions, support, and friendship.

We are indebted to the ongoing efforts of many colleagues, who are quietly at work around the country challenging people with opportunities for creative giving. And we also thank the folks at Discipleship Resources for their support in completing this project.

Cover design by Joey McNair
Interior design by PerfecType

ISBN 0-88177-470-7

Library of Congress Control Number 2004116739

DR470

Contents

Foreword

Creative Giving is a significant resource for every pastor and lay person seeking to know more about a dimension of Christian stewardship rarely discussed in churches today. *Creative Giving* discusses planned giving in a clear and compelling manner and boldly suggests that it is time for congregations to overcome *any* hesitancy to discuss gifts of accumulated assets by will, revocable trust, or other plan. In addition, *Creative Giving* provides an invaluable guide for building a marketing program that will ultimately lead church members to make planned gifts that will have a positive impact on church growth and life.

While planned giving has been the subject of other books, *Creative Giving* is specifically targeted to the unique needs of churches, making the case for establishing endowment funds to support congregational ministries.

Stories abound on how endowments have had a negative, rather than positive, influence on congregational life and growth. Many church leaders, irrespective of denomination, have stories to tell about how an endowed church gradually declined but could not die because an endowment provided artificial life support. *Creative Giving* tackles this concern head on, integrating theology, ethics, and other practical issues.

Creative Giving is inspiring and motivational, and it provides an easy-to-follow guide to help local church leadership plan for success. I recommend it to you wholeheartedly.

Charles Smith
Crystal Cathedral Ministries

CHAPTER 1

Introduction

C *reative Giving: Understanding Planned Giving and Endowments in Church* is the third and most challenging installment in the series of books about faith and money issues. *Faith & Money: Understanding Annual Giving in Church*[1] presents a broad common experience of the annual drive and the supporting theology. Most churches have some experience with addressing this kind of financial need, even if their experience is limited to whining about the church's operational needs.

Extraordinary Money! Understanding the Capital Campaign in Church[2] draws from a broad base of data from the last generation and offers a clear theological perspective. Many churches have discovered new vistas of financial experience through capital campaigns. While some churches can share horror stories about failed campaigns, a substantial number have found fundraising to be a spiritually and financially energizing experience.

It is in this third dimension of creative giving, however, where there are many opinions with little corroborating experience. In this area, there seem to be limited positive experiences, with anecdotal stories providing inconsistent views about the place and value of planned giving or church endowments. For the purposes of this book, we have used the more familiar terms of *planned giving* and *deferred giving* interchangeably with the term *creative giving*. It seems to us that this fresh description might bring some energy to the discussion, because we believe that many people have a benign reaction to the more familiar terms.

One school of thought maintains that the church has no business in planned giving because ministry ought to be funded through regular contributions. When a member dies and remembers the church in his or her will, however, few (if any) churches turn down the windfall.

There is also the often-heard story about how the existence of an endowment adversely affects regular giving. This is usually expressed in an anecdote about a church that received an extraordinary bequest and its negative impact on the ministry and spiritual vitality of the church.

Then there is the almost opposite view that it would be great if one person could endow the church so that the members did not have to give. Of course, this could not be the intent of a donor who was sensitive enough to make such a gift. Can you imagine the person who perceived the value in making an endowment to be that others could not have the same spiritual experience?

The problem with these stories is that there is enough truth in them to be alarming. The faith of a few churches around the country seems to be centered more in their enormous endowments than in the spiritual vitality of their churches.

Another reason this book is more difficult is because there is a lot of discussion about planned giving in nonprofit circles, including church and parachurch organizations, but much of the discussion stems from people selling some kind of supportive services for planned giving, from trust software to marketing resources, continuing education opportunities, and even academic programs. It is sometimes difficult to separate the marketing hype from the relevant, positive experience. Our research indicates that while there is some positive activity in planned giving, there is room for considerably more.

We also acknowledge that the initiative to write this book, as with the previous texts, might assume some sense of superior professional knowledge. We would like to share what we have experienced and learned, while we continue to learn. Our goal has been to develop a common starting place for understanding these issues, but we do not pretend to have an unusual sense of comfort with the subject matter. We have worked in this field for several years in a variety of settings, and we have experienced both encouraging and disappointing results. We hope that we can learn from each other.

The challenges facing most churches today are broad and significant. Even well-funded ministries must address the changing culture, membership declines, evolving values and priorities, and demographic shifts.

One common challenge is addressing spiritual values in an economy based on consumption. Researchers suggest that adults are exposed to thousands of commercial messages from the Internet, magazines, billboards, radio, television, movies, and home solicitation. In the midst of this economic landscape, the church, along with televangelists, seems to always be asking for money. The idea of connecting faith and money is more frequently seen as meeting the expanding financial needs of the church, and not the quality of the life of the disciple. Unfortunately, poor practice and false assumptions cause church leaders to serve the role of beggars, rather than serving the role of equipping saints to live a life worthy of the gospel of Christ.

Until recently, the church has focused almost exclusively on giving from cash flow and competing with consumer-driven marketing. Lately, however, there has been a shift. "Probably the greatest overall trend in protestant stewardship is the new emphasis on stewardship of wealth accumulated over the years by church members."[3]

Extraordinary Money explored the experience of capital campaigns in churches. While many of the multi-year commitments in a church capital campaign are based on cash flow, some of the most significant gifts come from accumulated assets. With the increased costs of capital development, including the costs of land and construction, churches have received more substantial gifts from accumulated assets. And while most nonprofit institutions have had annual fund drives, and quite a few have realized new levels of response in major gifts, many of these nonprofits have also provided strong experiences, thus validating the value of planned giving programs. Local churches, however, have struggled with this dimension of giving.

The purpose of this book is to explore the area of creative giving. We will attempt to identify the realities and debunk the myths concerning planned giving in churches. We will provide tools to analyze creative giving in the context of an individual community of faith.

The theology, philosophy, and ethical questions concerning this dimension of giving will be explored as well. The book will then identify the mediums of creative giving, including basic definitions of terms. Based on diverse experiences and solid research, we will present approaches to creative giving, including such issues as leadership roles, marketing samples, and recommended approaches for working with groups and individuals within the church. Finally, we will identify helpful resources and conclude with consideration of a financial master plan for local churches.

Throughout the book, we will share specific illustrations based on actual experiences in creative giving.

As local church leaders attempt to address the myriad of challenges they face in remaining relevant and effective in their many tasks, creative giving offers resources that can make a difference. Not only can these resources help the church financially, but they can also help mature saints for the work of the gospel and the pilgrimage of faith.

Somewhere along the way, we have come to an understanding that the accumulation of assets to assure a long, comfortable retirement is the goal of our life's work. Unfortunately, this view departs from the basic Christian theology of God's ownership of all that we possess. Retirement is not the problem; the problem is the attitude that is most often reflected when people say, "I can't give because I live on a fixed income." The reality is that many people who offer this response are well fixed and have forgotten who fixed them in the first place.

This attitude reflects a theology of scarcity, not abundance. The central issue in matters of faith and money is not the limitations we perceive, but the living out of our salvation as disciples obedient to a loving God who has provided for us. "Helping people with planned giving is a service to our members . . . [M]any people are unaware of how to use assets to support their Christian values and priorities."[4]

Notes

1. Michael D. Reeves and Jennifer Tyler, *Faith & Money: Understanding Annual Giving in Church* (Nashville: Discipleship Resources, 2003).

2. Michael D. Reeves, *Extraordinary Money! Understanding the Church Capital Campaign* (Nashville: Discipleship Resources, 2002).

3. From *Plain Talk About Churches and Money,* by Dean Hoge, Patrick McNamara, and Charles Zech, page 36. © 1997 The Alban Institute.

4. From *Afire with God: Spirit-ed Stewardship for a New Century,* by Betsy Schwarzentraub, page 64. © 2000 Discipleship Resources.

CHAPTER 2

Defining Realities and Debunking Myths

"In the next few years in the United States, we will experience the largest transfer of wealth between generations in history!" With the aging of the Baby Boomer generation and the passing of their parents, bold statements concerning this wealth transfer come from many sources. Depending on who is speaking and on the number of years projected, the amounts range into the trillions of dollars. The numbers are staggering.

Unfortunately, some assumptions are not necessarily accurate. Because of the size of this generational transfer of wealth, many have suggested that any nonprofit agency should receive its share if it just works at it. But there is little evidence to support this assumption.

Let's think about it logically. If you were going to consider the best use of your accumulated assets, would you really trust it to a nonprofit agency that was very small or only a few years old? Would you leave a significant gift to an agency whose purpose was not clear or whose leadership was not stable? Similarly, would you leave some of your accumulated assets to a church experiencing continuing internal conflict or declining in membership and attendance? Would you be comfortable leaving a gift to a church that had not effectively managed other bequests or that had not followed the donor's intentions? While every church needs an active annual stewardship program, and while many can benefit from a well-timed, well-led capital campaign, can we assume that every church should pursue planned gifts for its use?

One reality that needs to be defined is that senior adults, regardless of their accumulated wealth, often have an attitude that was shaped during the Depression. As adults or children of the Depression, a theology of scarcity is often a strong reality in their thinking. The illustration of one particular senior adult is reflective of this.

A few years ago at the age of eighty-five, one of our relatives was nearing the end of his life. He had outlived two wives and was residing in a moderately priced nursing home. He had to supplement his Medicare income to afford the nursing home, and during one of our last visits, he complained about his situation. He said to my wife and me, "This rest home is a nice place, but they're just after my money. I don't understand it. All I get here is my room, a television, a nurse, food, medication, and transportation, and they are charging me $61.00 a day more than the government is already paying them."

A few weeks later he passed away, and we discovered that in addition to his three-hundred-acre ranch, a home, a car, farm equipment, and a gas lease, he had $141,000.00 in his checking account and an uncashed check from the gas lease for $25,000.00. Despite all of these assets, he had a fear of running out of money! To approach a person like this who has the assets for a planned gift and to appropriately use the word *irrevocable* about a planned gift is, at best, a challenge.

Despite this illustration, and while the total amount of the generational transfer is substantial, there are a lot of recipients, and the average bequest is not as large as you might think. According to a study by the AARP, the average bequest in 2002 was $47,909.00.[1]

Another false assumption is that planned gifts are for the more affluent. The reality is that a planned gift is a creative way to enable people of modest means to make a significant gift. It is not unusual to read a story about a person of modest income, like a teacher, nurse, secretary, bus driver, or custodian, who leaves a substantial gift as a result of quiet investments made over a long period of years, from equity built up in a home, or from life insurance proceeds. Neither is it unusual to find a middle-aged professional with a six-figure annual income and significant accumulated assets who believes that planned gifts are for those more affluent individuals later in life.

For instance, when challenged to make planned gifts, the board members of one charitable organization provided interesting responses. Some with far more limited assets provided life insurance policy beneficiary designations, and others completed charitable gift annuities. One middle-aged professional, however, wrote a letter to the board chair and director complaining that planned gifts were for the rich and that he did not consider himself in that category. Another board member said that he might someday consider a planned gift, but at the moment he was remodeling his vacation condo and landscaping his primary home at the country club, and he was not in the position to make a planned gift. The prospect pool needs to be defined with a larger parameter than just the affluent in our society.

A subsequent chapter will address research, but how do we identify realistic expectations? With the number of not-for-profit agencies, institutions, churches, and parachurch organizations vying for planned gifts, and with an enormous potential for planned gifts in an affluent culture, is the potential for planned gifts being realized? The assumption that professionals in nonprofit agencies—including foundations, schools, colleges, hospitals, nonprofit associations, churches, and church agencies—are receiving significant numbers of planned gifts is just not supported by fact.

A recent survey of several church-related organizations whose defined purpose is the cultivation and solicitation of planned gifts in a particular geographic area produced interesting results. This group represented almost 6,000 churches with over 1,700,000 members and an average attendance of well over 600,000. In 2003, the first measurable area for planned giving analysis, these agencies had completed seventy-two charitable gift annuities, or one for almost 24,000 members. In an economic climate of low interest rates, you might expect the higher yields for gift annuity rates to be more appealing, but the results were, at best, limited.

The results for completed charitable remainder trusts were also alarming. In 2003, only eleven trusts were completed, representing one for every 156,000 members. When the results for a whole year by eight different agencies with a total of more than twenty staff members working on planned gifts can complete only one charitable gift annuity for every 79 churches and one charitable remainder trust for every 519 churches, the conclusion of unrealized potential is evident.[2]

Another assumption that should be debunked is the idea that a well-planned, well-executed giving program or a substantial endowment automatically has an adverse impact on operational giving. There are always examples of unusual situations where a substantial endowment or an individual gift had a deleterious effect on regular giving, but these exceptions are just that. The chapter on research will examine this empirically in more detail, but Eugene Grimm addresses a necessary guideline in his excellent book, *Generous People*:

> **Should the endowment fund be used to support the operating budget of the congregation?** The universal experience of congregations and church bodies says, "No!" There are two basic reasons: First, the common experience has been that this practice causes the members' financial support of the congregation to decline. . . . Second, such a practice discourages members from making gifts and bequests to endowment funds."[3]

So, a key decision is that the purposes of an endowment must be defined and communicated to the congregation to avoid any negative impact.

In a later chapter, we will consider purposes for endowments, but open communication is another issue that needs to be defined now. Some leaders believe that if the church endowment is communicated openly, then it could hurt the church. The time of the old leadership style of a few people holding the information "close to the vest" assumes that members today have institutional loyalty and trust in their leaders. Neither dimension of this assumption is true. Instead, according to research from the Alban Institute, the opposite is true:

> Most church leaders and institutions are secretive about what their endowments are and how they are used. The financial portion of a church's endowment needs to be fully public. There is no place for hiding resources. . . . There needs to be a strong dialogue among congregations and denominations about the use of such resources, and secretiveness muddies the discussion.[4]

One of the presuppositions for an effective planned giving program is to define the realities and debunk the myths about planned giving generally and specifically in the context of the local congregation. Chapter 5 provides an abundance of resources, but one remaining fundamental issue about planned giving in a local church is the development of a strategy that works in the context of a particular church. Many churches would be better served to not initiate a program for creative giving, because there are so many other distractions in their priorities. In their excellent article "Planned Giving for Churches: The Last Frontier?" John Foster and Derek Davis suggest that while congregation members give less of their disposable income to churches, "[i]t's the absence of a sustained planned giving program in most churches that really represents a missed opportunity."[5]

They believe that a lot of affluent people in churches are being approached for planned gifts from outside the church, and the church is not in the loop. While this is an accurate observation, it is the word *sustained* that is the problem. Churches have a lot of experience in surviving, but sustaining is different. Sustaining requires an intentional effort, an energy that is often missing in a church culture that tends to be reactionary rather than proactive. Can a church be successful in a planned giving program? Yes, if there is a will to succeed, but the will and energy necessary to sustain a program is rarely observed.

Notes

1. Glenn Ruffenach, "The Great American Retirement Quiz," *The Wall Street Journal*, December 20, 2004, Section R, page 3.

2. Jurisdictional research.

3. From *Generous People: How to Encourage Vital Stewardship*, by Eugene Grimm, page 148. © 1992 Abingdon Press.

4. From *Financial Meltdown in the Mainline?*, by Loren Mead, page 96. © 1998. The Alban Institute.

5. From "Planned Giving for Churches: The Last Frontier?" by John Foster and Derek Davis, *Planned Giving Today*, January 2002.

PERMANENT FUND FACTS

Do Churches Benefit from Creative Giving?

"Endowments have a positive effect on regular giving in mainline churches . . ."

From *Financial Meltdown in the Mainline?*, by Loren Mead.
© 1998 The Alban Institute.

"Endowment funds increase per member contributions."

From *The People(s) Called Methodist*, by Charles Zech,
page 94. © 1998 Abingdon Press.

When a church opens the doors of planned giving (giving from one's accumulation) *at least five things will happen.*

1. The church will receive increased gifts to fund various ministries.
2. Members will begin to examine their Christian stewardship concepts and understandings in a broader context and will begin to include planned gifts as well as current gifts in their stewardship response.
3. Members will be educated about the many gift opportunities for mission and ministry through their church.
4. Current contributions given in support of the ongoing annual budget will be freed up to strengthen and even expand existing programs.
5. The church and its various ministries and institutions will begin to receive major planned gifts that have previously been directed to other causes where planned-giving programs are already in place.

From *Creating a Climate for Giving*, by Donald Joiner,
page 77 © 2001 Discipleship Resources.

"Planned gifts can increase the success of a capital campaign. . . . Planned giving looks at options and opportunities that might allow a donor to make a planned gift even though he lacks current funds with which to make a capital campaign gift."

From *Getting Started in Planned Giving*, by Kathryn W. Miree, page 5. © 1999 Kathryn Miree Associates.

How many congregations do some planned giving?

Budgets over $200,000	59%
Budgets between $100K and $200K	59%
Budgets under $100,000	39%

From *How to Increase Giving in Your Church*, by George Barna, page 102. © 1994 Regal Books.

"Charities that have actively encouraged gifts via estates are now experiencing sustained growth rates of 15 percent or more annually."

From *Give and Take*, Volume 32, No. 8, page 1. © 2000 Robert F. Sharpe & Co.

Why Do Donors Give?

"Endowments open doors to wider mission opportunities."

From "Endowed Congregations: Pros and Cons," by Loren Mead, page 5 © 1998 The Alban Institute.

"Some members are inclined to give an endowment fund, whereas they wouldn't give to an annual budget; therefore, having an endowment increases overall giving."

From *Plain Talk about Churches and Money*, by Dean Hoge, Patrick McNamara, and Charles Zech, page 109. © 1997 The Alban Institute.

"Successful churches that receive a number of planned gifts offer frequent teaching seminars and mailings regarding the variety of possibilities members should consider as good stewards of their resources."

> From *Holy $moke! Whatever Happened to Tithing?*,
> by J. Clif Christopher and Herb Mather, page 78.
> © 2001 Discipleship Resources.

"Studies show that approximately 85 percent of those who have made a planned gift will make another one—either to your institution or somewhere else."

> From *Wit, Wisdom & Moxie*, by Jerold Panas, page 96.
> © 2002 Bonus Books.

"Surprisingly, tax considerations do not significantly influence wealthy Americans' penchant for charitable giving. Ninety-five percent of those surveyed said they would still make charitable contributions, even if they were not tax-deductible."

> From "U.S. Trust Survey of Affluent Americans,"
> November 1998 © U.S. Trust.

"One more thing of particular interest. Those who provide for charity in their estate plans live longer that the general public—six years beyond the Actuarial Tables."

> From *Wit, Wisdom & Moxie*, by Jerold Panas, page 154.
> © 2002 Bonus Books.

Who Are Donors?

In their best-selling book, *The Millionaire Next Door*, Stanley and Danko describe millionaires as the people next door who live in modest homes, drive three-year-old cars, and rarely take expensive vacations—the perfect portrait of many church members.

"For the 'average' family in most congregations, only 15 percent of its net worth is current income; 85 percent of its net worth is accumulated resources."

> From *Generous People: How to Encourage Vital Stewardship*, by
> Eugene Grimm, page 119. © 1992 Abingdon Press.

"Eight-two percent of affluent parents are concerned about instilling in their children the importance of being involved in charity."

From "U.S. Trust Survey of Affluent Americans,"
November 1998 © U.S. Trust.

"Here's what we know: if you ask your donor base to give a second time during the year, 40 percent will. Try it."

From *Wit, Wisdom & Moxie*, by Jerold Panas, page 146.
© 2002 Bonus Books.

CHAPTER 3

A Resilient and Faithful Theology

E ven though there is no specific, definitive biblical teaching about planned giving, we are not left without guidance for understanding scriptural relevance in the faithful management of the resources that God provides. A scriptural foundation and theological framework for general Christian stewardship was formulated in the companion to this book, *Faith and Money*. These principles are certainly applicable in understanding the importance of the faithful management of our accumulated assets in our personal and familial estates. Certainly the economic and cultural conditions are different between this era and the broad interval that is referred to as "biblical times." We would be unwise, however, to assume that many of the current widely held cultural attitudes and philosophical formulations are faithfully shaped by biblical teachings or by historic theological perspectives.

In understanding our biblical heritage and applying its relevance to the area of creative giving, we can begin with the clarity that God is depicted in many scriptural passages as a giving Being. This is perhaps clearer nowhere than in the passage every child who grew up in the church memorized at an early age: "For God so loved the world . . . " (John 3:16). This is the guideline we have before us as we attempt to live our lives "in a godly fashion." The dynamics of creative giving embody a deep and earnest desire to be faithful with all that God gives for our use and management.

Leviticus 25 provides an ancient Hebrew understanding that came forth from the Lord's directives to Moses on Mount Sinai. It describes every fiftieth year as a hallowed interval of jubilee. Because the land is God's and the people are aliens and tenants, everyone is called by the Lord's directive to provide for the redemption of the land. This fifty-year interval would have approximated an individual's life span, and instructions are given for passing or recovering land at that time. Since it is God's land and cannot be taken by its inhabitants, the distribution of property was to be done in accordance with the directives for faithfulness in living and in dying. The concept, then, of transferring property has a longstanding place in the Judeo-Christian tradition, and its purpose is to faithfully honor God.

While Jesus provided many instructions in the New Testament on managing the resources God provides, the relevance to what we call planned giving is certainly evident in the parable of the talents (Matthew 25:14-30). The fearful one who buried the asset that had been provided to him was scoffed, reprimanded, and condemned to "the outer darkness." The others who managed well that which was provided were rewarded. They used what had been provided, they grew it, and they returned it with glad and faithful hearts to the one who had provided it. How we use that which is provided and how we make it grow—so that the work of God can expand and grow—determine the faithfulness of our response and the reward that will be provided.

When Paul wrote Timothy, whom he called his "loyal child in the faith," he urged the younger man to command those who are rich "to set their hopes on God who richly provides us with everything for our enjoyment." Paul goes further to declare that "they are to do good, to be rich in good works, generous, and ready to share, thus storing up for themselves the treasure of a good foundation for the future, so that they may take hold of the life that really is life" (1 Timothy 6:17-19). Paul calls them to invest in the kingdom yet to come, and, in so doing, they establish a firm foundation for that which is yet to be.

One final scriptural passage worthy of note is Psalm 100, which combines several of these themes: the origin of all by God, the urgency of responsive praise and worship, and the steadfastness of God across the generations. There is a further emphasis—that of thanksgiving, of deep and abiding gratitude. Humble gratitude invites us to honor God through the gifts that God has given us for the good of this generation and those to come.

The emphases of these passages allow us to develop a theology that can guide personal, familial, and congregational considerations and decisions about creative giving. That which has been given to us for a short interval is from God, and we are in a unique position to use it to glorify God in this and the coming generations.

With this biblical and theological perspective in mind, several aspects of the cultural philosophical momentum must be noted and addressed. We grasp the idea of passing our assets along from one generation to another, but we forget the balancing part of the message about doing good with that which has been provided. Let me illustrate.

My wife and I are the beneficiaries of our parents' lifetime estates. While their accumulated assets are not huge, our parents believe that leaving something to their children is their responsibility. Part of this attitude comes from their Depression-era upbringing, and part comes from their winsome notion of the American Dream. They have worked hard, managed well, and saved. Their accumulated assets will be passed on.

This view of ownership, however, is in conflict with some of the most basic tenets of faith. If the accumulated assets belong to God, and if we are managers of those assets, is the cultural momentum theologically sound? It is the confusion around this issue of ownership that needs to be unraveled.

John Wesley's assertion that you should not leave your assets to your offspring unless they are good stewards should be reexamined in our contemporary culture. Wesley's comment seems harsh, because it is so countercultural. That is the very point: of what core significance are your spiritual beliefs? Most significant spiritual movements in history were countercultural. Redefining the issue of ownership, the nature of stewardship, and the American Dream requires a clear understanding of what we really believe and why.

The theology of stewardship suggested in *Faith and Money* expresses that God is the source—the owner of all we have—and those accumulated assets are not excluded. Another theological theme is also important: giving is a part of discipleship.

In our consumptive culture, there are a great number of reasons people give for poor stewardship. A perception of scarce resources is a common one. The interesting dichotomy of accumulated assets is the frequent response, "I am on a fixed income." The truth is that a lot of people who use this line are well fixed, and the central problem is their understanding of ownership.

Many people demonstrate more faith in their investment portfolios than they do in God's provisions. (One only wonders how shaky their faith was during the bear market of 2001 and 2002!) The difficulty has its roots in the popular theology of scarcity and in the failure to grow year after year in trust of God's capacity to create, provide, sustain, and continue.

The insidiousness of this theology of scarcity allows it to pervade congregational identity as well as personal attitudes. During a recent visit with church leaders of a middle-class suburban church, one of the financial leaders was bothered by the mission support expected of the church by denominational leaders. It was recognized that two years before, mission education had been very intentional, and the full mission support had been paid. In the previous year, however, only 19 percent had been paid, because the focus on mission education had waned.

The leader said that he was unclear about what "all that money went for" but challenged that they should ask those receiving the funds if they would rather get the money or have the church pay the electric bill. The idea that there was a limited amount of money, combined with poor education and a fundamental loss of purpose, resulted in a shifting focus away from divine calling and mission to nothing more than comfort and survival.

The irony was that this meeting was only a few days after the devastation of the December 2004 tsunami, which was being extensively and graphically reported. One person observed that perhaps the need to pay the electric bill was less of a priority than basic food and medical care for South Asia. The resulting dialogue was animated, and there was agreement that intentional education would likely result in more positive and more generous giving.

The same theology of scarcity that brought about the conversation in this church is evident in other churches that persistently express more faith in the stock market or an endowment than they do in God's provision. Significant progress has been made in many churches in the areas of annual and capital giving, but few churches have been effective in providing a consistent program for planned giving.

An underlying factor leading to this inability to initiate strong creative giving programs is fear, which, unfortunately, inhibits much of our financial stewardship leaders. A primary fear seems to be the possibility of offending people.

While this fear is evident to some degree in annual and capital giving, it seems more pronounced in planned giving. The strength of the cultural momentum for the obligatory passing of our assets to select family members and the confusion of ultimate ownership of our accumulated assets overwhelm us and undermine our confidence.

To complicate the matter further, we also face challenges with members of my parents' generation, influenced by poignant memories of the Depression, who relentlessly cling to safety nets of resources "just in case." Subsequent generations do not seem to have the same anxiety, at least not as acutely as my parents' and grandparents' generations do.

This same fear dynamic can be seen in the church's decisions about endowments. As one pastor expressed it, "I want our church to live by faith, but it is much easier when we have endowment income just in case." In case of what? In case God really doesn't provide? In case the people of God fail to be financially faithful?

Another powerful fear is that an endowment will automatically have an adverse effect on regular giving. There are some examples where this is true, but they are anecdotal at best. A huge unrestricted or narrowly designated endowment can have a substantial negative impact on regular giving, but this is rare.

One church blessed with such an endowment planned and maintained a budget in which less than half of the income came from contributions, and the larger portion came from endowment distributions. Capital needs were addressed from the endowment earnings as well. The net result was a congregation (hardly eligible to be called a community of faith) that did not encourage people to mature in their discipleship through stewardship. This, however, is the exception, not the rule.

Is it even logical that a donor or donors who leave substantial sums to a church intend for people to give less? Gift-acceptance policies that define clear uses and open communication about church endowments can eliminate these issues before they become a problem, and these steps will be offered in subsequent chapters of this book.

There are numerous illustrations of healthy churches that have developed endowments created by individual planned gifts that indefinitely perpetuate personal or familial annual pledges. Typically, these have been designated for deferred maintenance, scholarships, or missional opportunities.

Research on the impact of endowments on regular giving consistently shows that regular giving is enhanced by a well-planned and consistently

administered deferred giving program. Therefore, the theology of fear
must be challenged and dismantled by the evidence—stories that emerge
from churches whose programs have not only added deep personal satisfaction to its members' lives, but have also brought financial strength to
congregations for the fulfillment of their divinely given call to do God's
work in the world.

It is the grounding in biblical understanding and the development of a
sturdy theological framework that provide the capacity to build effective
creative giving programs and to overcome some of the culturally powerful
and fearfully motivated attitudes that exist in our day. Biblical sources help
us form a belief system that is more relevant and more enduring than mere
cultural attitudes and popular reason.

In First Chronicles, Chapter 29, David says that in support of the building of the Temple, he is making a gift "over and above" his regular giving
from his "treasury." The treasury could be defined as his accumulated
assets. And in Second Corinthians, Chapter 8, Paul suggests that liberality
in giving comes from a spiritual priority: ". . . they first gave themselves to
the Lord. . . ." We need not be shy or ill-equipped to preach and teach in
such a way that the hearts and minds of our people are brought to
new—and biblically faithful—understandings of God's provisions!

CHAPTER 4

Ethical Considerations

We worship in a beautiful downtown structure of a mainline-denomination church, which was established in 1835 on Church Street. The cornerstone of the building was laid in 1925.

It was a hard time to build a new church. The old building had been sold, and construction began on the new one. As the times grew harder, the bank became uneasy with many loans, including the one for the church. It appeared that the new building would also have to be sold to pay off the loan unless individual members of the church believed strongly enough in its future to personally guarantee payment. They did, and the first service took place on March 30, 1926.

Today, it is an easy place in which to worship. The backdrop to the altar is a majestic cross. Beautiful stained-glass windows adorn each wall. The rich wood grains of the pews, rails, and altar are warm and inviting. The air conditioning keeps us cool in the summer, and the heat keeps us warm in the winter. Even the cushions are comfortable.

If you had been looking for me on a Sunday morning during the last several years, all you would have needed to do was come to my church. Walk from the rear toward the front right part of the sanctuary, and look for our "family pew." It is our family pew because of our habit of sitting in the same place each Sunday. The odds are you would find my parents, my children, my wife, and me all sitting together.

On each end of the wooden pews are brass nameplates in recognition of the donors who provided for them. Ironically, the names that appear are not ours. Countless times I have offered silent prayers of thanks for those who provided three generations of my family with a place to sit and worship our God together. Those members in the Depression who stepped up to the first loan and those whose names appear on the brass plaques surely knew that they could attend another church that did not have the same financial needs. Why did they do what they did?

Earnest Campbell, pastor of Riverside Church in New York City, has been credited with a piece that may answer the question.

Understanding Maturity

To be young is to study in schools we did not build.
To be mature is to build schools in which we will not study.

To be young is to swim in pools we did not dig.
To be mature is to dig pools in which we will not swim.

To be young is to sit under trees, which we did not plant.
To be mature is to plant trees under which we will not sit.

To be young is to dance to music we did not write.
To be mature is to write music to which we will not dance.

To be young is to worship in churches we did not build.
To be mature is to build churches in which we may not worship.[1]

Some of the past members of our church understood maturity of stewardship, but we no longer need to purchase pews for the congregation. Does that lessen our obligation to provide for the future of the church? More importantly to us, shall it deny us the opportunity to give the abundant blessings that God has bestowed on us to continue his work in the kingdom? What is left for us? Must we move to a newer or poorer church to be given a chance to "mature"?

Creative giving, giving from one's accumulated resources, provides a unique opportunity to mature. The church will need to maintain the building, replace volunteer staff with paid staff, and establish new areas of ministry. But it is not the church's need for our gifts that is important; it is our need to give—our need to spiritually mature.

The economies of the world continue to change. Material wealth used to be measured in terms of crops or flocks. It was only natural to use these same assets as offerings to thank God for abundantly providing. In the early days of our country, the average American thought in terms of immediate survival, a day-to-day existence. The world economy evolved from one of bartered goods to one of monetary exchange to a consumer-driven economy involving substantial vehicles of debt.

Most contemporary churches do not feel comfortable talking about money. So they don't. This discomfort ignores the biblical evidence about our relationship with money, including the recurring theme of Jesus' parables about our relationship with our stuff. Today's world is full of an ever-changing array of financial products and services.

As the graying of America has found its way into church congregations, new questions arise. Older members are often some of the most loyal and generous supporters of the faith. As their walk on earth comes to an end, how does the church help them conclude their stewardship journey in a manner pleasing to God? Does not the way their accumulated assets are used say something about their values and their faith? How does the church not appear self-serving by encouraging creative gifts?

One ethical concern seems to be the worry of being perceived as a salesperson. The ability to sell an idea, concept, product, or way of life, however, is a gift just like any other. Actually, it is a combination of gifts.

One is the ability to be sensitive and caring enough to want to learn how you can help someone in need. Another is the ability to understand the possible methods available to address that need. Yet another is the ability to communicate articulately how the need can be met with the methods available—for the benefit of all involved. It is all about relationships and meeting needs.

A doctor asks questions to determine symptoms, which will identify the patient's malady so that a treatment may be prescribed. An attorney ascertains the facts of a case to determine the legal strategy to use. A counselor seeks to understand the causes of the problem before offering advice. All of these professionals have to develop relationships with their patients or clients in order to ask the questions that will help them make appropriate recommendations. A planned giving professional must do the same thing.

The questions to ask are those that flow naturally when we develop a relationship with anyone. Tell me about your family. What are your thoughts and dreams about their future? Do you have siblings, children, or grandchildren whom you would like to help? Do you have a special ministry or charity that you have helped during your lifetime that you would like to continue to help after you are gone? What is your current financial situation? Who are the financial professionals helping you with your affairs?

Creative giving provides a way for people to make mature gifts. Many of the vehicles used in creative giving, some of which will be described in a later chapter, are a form of deferred gift. One can make an irrevocable commitment now to meet the spiritual need, yet continue to benefit from the assets God has provided. Such gifts may appear complicated to donors, but involving their financial advisors should help. Written illustrations and encouraging questions are helpful in this conversation. Any worthwhile gift should be able to stand both the test of time and the light of day.

Another recurring ethical consideration of creative giving is whether the local church should be considered a possible recipient for such gifts. Frankly, the answer is not easy. The wonderful church buildings we sit in today were provided by a previous generation to help support the ministry of the church. There are, however, many churches whose default mission is survival and facility maintenance. Is this default mission really worthy of a planned gift to provide some kind of support in perpetuity? And taking a long look is very difficult. What will the church's place be in the community or in mission in ten, twenty, or fifty years in the future?

This issue is addressed in detail from a historical perspective in Lyle Schaller's book *The New Context for Ministry*.[2] In *The Present Future*, Reggie McNeal observes that the church structure we have known during our lifetime is rapidly collapsing.[3] Are we really more concerned with historical preservation of the facilities? Are there better ways to provide for meeting human need? Today, you can tour Europe and find wonderful, historic architecture that seems spiritually devoid. It is more of a monument to spiritual fervor of the past.

Perhaps it is a question of leadership. Can an endowment be properly managed and distributed by current and future leaders? There are ample examples of leaders not observing the intent of a donor's bequest throughout the church. With a default survival mission, rationalization is not a difficult second step down a slippery slope of misuse of endowed funds. Is the enormous fixed expense of a physical facility what God had in mind for the church? A third-party manager and secondary beneficiary seem to be desirable for a broader view of respecting the donor's intent.

Recently, a church-related college was facing some financial challenges. With enrollment down, a bear market, and debt, they tried to develop a financial strategy. They did not focus their mission on being a liberal arts university competing with state-funded schools, but rather asked their legal counsel to review restricted funds to see whether their donors or their heirs were still alive, so that some of the restrictions could be redefined in light of the current need.

Whether a building is underutilized or an endowment fund is misused, it remains our responsibility to be good and faithful stewards of all of God's gifts. The challenge is not the structure or form of the asset; it is our ability to assist the donor in discerning God's purpose for its use.

Notes

1. Ernest Campbell, "Understanding Maturity." Used by permission of the author.

2. Lyle Schaller, *The New Context for Ministry: Competing for the Charitable Dollar* (Nashville: Abingdon Press, 2002).

3. Reggie McNeal, *The Present Future: Six Tough Questions for the Church* (San Francisco: Jossey-Bass, 2003).

CHAPTER 5

Research and Resources

While financial stewardship is a historically significant issue, creative giving is relatively new. Since biblical times, tithes and offerings have been taught and illustrated. Annual and building campaigns have a long track record that can be discussed and analyzed. The issue of the stewardship of accumulated assets, however, is a more recent consideration.

Beginning with the great wealth generated during the Industrial Revolution, people such as Carnegie, Mellon, and Rockefeller have considered the value of philanthropy during or after life. But the church has struggled with the issue from several points of reference.

First, with the increase of wealth in the United States, the explosion of discretionary income and accumulated assets has begged the question, should the church have an endowment? Second, since the assets are substantial and the culture has experienced diminished institutional and denominational loyalty, many denominational leaders feel that this form of stewardship should be committed to denominational needs. And third, church institutions lay claim to planned gifts as significant funding sources for their futures. There is no shortage of opinions about the value or the designation of this source of revenue.

Unfortunately, varied opinions led to inconsistent results and very little agreement about priorities or appropriate approaches in the area of deferred giving. Then some significant research began about the place of both deferred giving and endowments in church life. Through grants funded by the Lilly Endowment and related organizations like the Alban Institute, research and articles started to emerge. Several of them merit attention.

Eugene Grimm offers a clear voice on the subject in his excellent book, *Generous People: How to Encourage Vital Stewardship.*[1] In Appendix E, "Questions for an Endowment/Trust Fund," he suggests that planned gifts in the church are good. They should not, however, support the budget. Grimm goes further to give guidance regarding governance and communication about such funds.

A comprehensive presentation is made in two undated Alban Institute articles: "Endowed Congregations: Pros and Cons," by Loren Mead,[2] and "Congregational Endowment Funds: Empowering the Vision of God's Coming Kingdom," by Gerald W Bauer.[3] Both articles address and expand on some of the same issues as Grimm. Mead expanded his thoughts even more in his 1998 book, *Financial Meltdown in the Mainline?*[4]

All of these efforts agreed on some fundamental issues:

- There is a place for planned giving in the local church.
- An endowment should not supplement operational revenue.
- The purpose of endowment distributions should be defined.
- The endowment should be openly communicated.
- The impact on regular giving is negligible.
- The effort should be intentional and well planned.

In 1996, one of the most significant research projects was published. Funded by a Lilly Endowment grant, John and Sylvia Ronsvalle provided keen analysis and empirical research in their excellent work, *Behind the Stained Glass Windows: Money Dynamics in the Church.*[5] In their research, the Ronsvalles consider the issue of the impact of an endowment on regular giving. Quoting Mead's work, along with denominational leaders, they conclude that gift-acceptance policies that define specific uses for the fund can substantially reduce negative consequences.

In 1997, another Lilly-funded research effort was published through the Alban Institute: *Plain Talk about Churches and Money.*[6] Dean Hoge, Patrick McNamara, and Charles Zech offered interesting empirical analysis in their chapter entitled "Church Invested Funds." Their research found that a very small number of churches had endowments of more than $100,000.00, and very few of them were investment-dependent.

This research and the related publications address the fears often expressed about the place of deferred giving and endowments in the local church. Overall, the net impact is positive.

The observations by Hoge, McNamara, and Zech have an inverse effect as well. With so much wealth and so few results, the potential is enormous. This was also validated by a recent survey alluded to in Chapter 2 of this book. In one judicatory area in one year, the institutions charged with promoting planned giving and endowments in the local church had experienced only seventy-two charitable gift annuities and eleven charitable remainder trusts in 5,712 churches with 1, 711,561 members in eight states. With twenty-two staff members working this field, it would seem that there is substantial potential.[7]

An abundance of helpful resources can be used in planned giving and endowments in the local church. One thing that becomes apparent in this research is the need for an organized, consistent approach to planned giving. A number of churches have a myriad of programs and challenges, and integrating another priority into a withering schedule requires more energy than many seem to have. Don Joiner addresses this in a concise consideration of planned giving in his book, *Creating a Climate for Giving*.[8] In Chapter 7, Joiner not only provides a basic understanding of planned giving, but also provides a detailed five-year plan for implementing a planned giving program in church.

Additional resources could include those provided by a denominational or judicatory agency dedicated to planned giving or endowments. The caution is that these denominational resources vary in quality and purpose. In this book, we have identified a number of excellent resources in other books, many of which provide additional bibliographies, which in turn offer stories, forms, approaches, and lists of resources for review. For example, in his book, *Wealth in Families*, Charles Collier offers eleven pages of additional resources.[9]

Professional organizations are another excellent outlet for resources. The National Committee on Planned Giving, the Association of Fundraising Professionals, the Ecumenical Center for Stewardship Studies, and the Christian Stewardship Association have all been helpful at various times during our work in this area. And, of course, there are a host of resources available on the Internet.

One last encouragement about resources is the value of other professionals in this work. Some of the best information comes from church leaders, who may have never published or shared what succeeds for them in their settings. This kind of communication can provide a wealth of relevant, helpful information.

Other studies are available, but the resources identified here helped shape our thinking and supported our experiences in this area. The few negative stories can be balanced by positive ones, and the research is substantial. It shows that there is a place for planned giving in the local church. The most relevant research is that which can be done in your own church using the tools for analysis identified in the next chapter.

Notes

1. Grimm, *Generous People*.

2. Loren Mead, "Endowing Congregations: Pros and Cons" (Special Papers and Research Reports, Alban Institute, n.d.).

3. Gerald Bauer, "Congregational Endowment Funds: Empowering the Vision of God's Coming Kingdom," (Special Papers and Research Reports, Alban Institute, n.d.).

4. Mead, *Financial Meltdown in the Mainline?.*

5. John and Sylvia Ronsvalle, *Behind the Stained Glass Windows: Money Dynamics in the Church* (Grand Rapids: Baker Books, 1996).

6. Hoge, McNamara, and Zech, *Plain Talk About Churches and Money*.

7. Jurisdictional research.

8. Don Joiner, *Creating a Climate for Giving* (Nashville: Discipleship Resources, 2001).

9. Charles W. Collier, *Wealth in Families* (Cambridge: Harvard University, 2002).

CHAPTER 6

Analytical Questions

Planned giving requires the decision to act by both the ministries receiving the gifts and the donors making them. In our consumer-driven economy, it is only natural to begin by asking, "What's in it for me?"

The Ministry

Most ministries feel their needs are growing while their resources seem to be shrinking. It seems almost counterintuitive to add yet another thing to do. Why bother with another aspect of the touchy topic of money?

Because the spiritual needs in the world are as strong today as ever, and no one seems to think that they will decrease in the future. Competition for the hearts and minds of people, however, increases every day.

In his book, *Mustard Seed versus McWorld*, Tom Sine describes the challenge as "a global macromall in which the wealthy and those of us on the middle rungs have been presented with an incredible and exploding array of consumer choice."[1] As proof, he cites the three thousand commercial messages most of us are confronted with in any twenty-four-hour period.

Perhaps in an effort to respond to these marketing messages, it appears that more families rely on dual incomes and, as the Harris Poll reports, Americans are working longer hours (fifty-one hours in 1997 versus forty-one in 1973).[2]

Yet, the need for the peace of Christ has never been greater. How will we address these spiritual challenges in the future? How do we replace the volunteer workers who have entered the workplace? How will we afford to maintain the facilities built by past donors without cannibalizing the mission projects that deal directly with problems that appeal to younger generations?

Building endowments through planned giving can provide a solution, but the window of opportunity will not be open indefinitely. Analysis begins by asking some critical questions.

Did anyone die in your church last year?

In most of the mainline churches I visit, heads are covered with gray or white hair, if anything at all. These members of "The Greatest Generation" are disappearing. One projection indicates deaths among World War II veterans will peak in 2008 at a level of 620,000.[3] How many did your ministry lose last year?

Did they remember the church in their estate plans?

Much is written about the great intergenerational transfer of wealth, indicating that these people had some measure of wealth. Did your ministry receive any such gifts last year?

How much has your bequest income grown?

Gifts by bequest grew nationally by 153 percent in the ten years from 1993 to 2003. According to Giving USA 2004, bequest giving in 2003 was $21.6 billion, up almost 13 percent from the 2002 total of $19.2 billion.[4] Did you receive any gift through a bequest last year? Was it more than the year before?

How do you ask to be remembered in estate plans?

Do you even ask? The reason we are given most often for people not including their churches in their wills is that they have not been asked. Why not? A recent study investigating the best methods to use and the best people to ask revealed that nearly all individuals included in the study felt it was appropriate for charities to solicit bequest gifts.

Other nonprofits aren't shy about asking. And their numbers are growing daily. The January 6, 2005, issue of *The Chronicle of Philanthropy* reported that nearly 800,000 charities are now listed on the

Internal Revenue Service's official roster.[5] Universities, libraries, and even the magazine *Consumer Reports* asks their constituents to make planned gifts to support their efforts.

How do we teach our people about bequests?

Probably the second most common excuse for not including churches in wills is lack of knowledge. People feel their estates are too small, the process is too expensive, or they just don't want to think about death. What safer place could there be than your ministry to learn the facts about estate planning?

How many faithful givers in our church are over the age of seventy?

One of the blessings of our era is extended lifetimes. Over 90 percent of bequests come from people who live past the age of seventy.[6] Does your church have many people over this age? Have you looked to see how many of them are consistent financial supporters of your ministry? Doesn't their support indicate the value they place on your work? Why would they think it would not be valuable in the future? What would be the effect of losing their support?

Does our church have any widows or widowers?

By definition, widows and widowers have reached the point in their lives where they no longer need to worry about providing for their spouses. While they may have other family members to consider, they certainly have lessened responsibilities.

Do we have sermons or testimonies about creative giving throughout the year?

How do any of us learn about any topic? We have to be exposed to the subject. Educators have long promoted the advantage of repetition in the learning process.

Do we make published material on the subject available?

Thirty-four percent of donors credit their charity's published material as the initial source of the idea of giving.[7]

Are any of our members with a desire to give concerned about income?

A life income gift is a gift vehicle designed to provide the donor with an income stream for a set number of years or for his or her entire lifetime.

How do we teach stewardship of accumulated assets?

Are the biblical guides on sharing our blessings with others limited to current income streams? What about increases in the values of stock portfolios, investment real estate, and retirement plans?

How do we educate our members about creative giving?

"You are an answer to prayer" was one lady's comment after a presentation at her church. "I know I need to do something, but everyone I talk to has something to sell." What better place to learn?

Who in your ministry is responsible for stewardship education?

What do you have planned or scheduled to help address this need?

(These last two questions should move you to act. If you can answer them, you are on your way.)

The Donor

The United States Census Bureau's most recent numbers describe the average American family, or consumer unit, as containing 2.5 persons and two vehicles. The average income is near $50,000.00, and 67.9 percent of us own our own homes.[8]

The Millionaire Next Door, by Thomas Stanley and William Danko, first exposed us to the idea that it is not the highly paid athlete or movie star who dominates the ranks of the well-to-do. Instead, it is hard-working individuals with traditional values living modest lifestyles. Seventy-five percent are reported to have never spent more than $599.00 on a suit or more than $199.00 on a pair of shoes. Ninety percent of their wealth is realized from assets growing untaxed, rather than from income.[9]

How would we describe the people sitting around us in church? Are they not "average"? They probably live in average three-bedroom houses with spouses and children and drive average four-year-old cars. Most of their wealth is probably from their assets as well.

While they may be very grateful to God for their blessings, they may find it hard to make mature gifts from their cash flows. It is a good service, if not a true ministry, to help them understand how they can make planned gifts.

Can They Afford It?

What is your supporters' potential? One of the easiest ways of understanding your congregation's potential is to research its average household income or its average net worth. Several sources provide average income and net worth data for particular ZIP Codes. The local chamber of commerce or the school district often has this information, and they use it for their business and development plans. Using publicly available statistical information helps counteract a negative theology of scarcity, which suggests that few people have available resources.

Donative Intent

"Honey," she said, "that church has been an important part of my husband's and my life, and we want to do something significant for all that it gave us."

Why is it hard for us to believe that people served by the church for a lifetime want to give back from their accumulated blessings? Members should include their churches as beneficiaries of their estates. It should be as natural as remembering spouses and natural heirs as beneficiaries. Members' estate plans should reflect who they are and who they have become during their lifetimes.

Estate planning professionals often start with a questionnaire on which clients list assets, liabilities, and the individuals and institutions they wish to make beneficiaries of their estates. Most secular advisors do not ask, "Would you like to remember the church, which has fed you and your family spiritually during your lifetime?"

Shouldn't we?

Notes

1. From *Mustard Seed versus McWorld: Reinventing Life and Faith for the Future*, by Tom Sine, page 88. © 1999 Baker Book House Company.

2. *Ibid.*, 92.

3. *The Vets to Washington Project*, January 11, 2005, http://www.vetstowashington.com

4. Giving USA 2004, "The Annual Report on Philanthropy for the Year 2004," 49th Annual Issue, researched and written at the Center on Philanthropy at Indiana University (AAFRC Trust for Philanthropy, 2003), page 66.

5. *Chronicle of Philanthropy*, January 6, 2005.

6. Planned Giving in the US, 2000.

7. *Ibid*.

8. *Downtown San Diego Properties*, April 22, 2005, www.downtownsandiegoproperties.com/home_ownership.htm.

9. Thomas Stanley and William Danko, *The Millionaire Next Door: The Surprising Secrets of America's Wealthy* (Atlanta: Longstreet Press, 1996), page 32.

CREATIVE GIVING POTENTIAL

"But you don't understand; our people are not rich."

"For every forty giving units in a church, one unit is capable of making a one-time gift equal to the church's annual budget."

From *Money Is Everything*, by Herb Miller, page 54.
© 1997 Discipleship Resources.

"For the 'average' family in most congregations, only 15 percent of its net worth is current income; 85 percent of its net worth is accumulated resources."

From *Generous People: How to Encourage Vital Stewardship*,
by Eugene Grimm, page 119.
© 1992 Abingdon Press.

Zip Code	Income	# Units	Net Worth[*]	Collective Potential
70124	$84,884	60	$565,893	$33,953,580
70005	$75,421	30	$502,807	$5,084,180
70001	$54,282	20	$361,880	$7,231,600
70003	$61,299	10	$408,660	$4,086,600
				50,355,960

[*]*Based on 2000 census actual income averages and Grimm's assertion.*

What if all 120 members tithed their estate? A tithe of the collective potential estate value would be $5,035,596.00. An endowment of $5,035,596.00 earning 3 percent would generate $151,068.00 per year.

LEGACY QUESTIONNAIRE

Legacies reflect who we are and what we hold dear. We use our experience and wisdom to benefit those we love and who love us. It is the method by which we make a life statement by leaving something behind. Beneficiaries often include spouses, children, grandchildren, friends, and universities. What about our church?

How do I want to be remembered?
What are my values?
What aspects of my life do I find to be most important?
How do I choose to be remembered?
From where did my blessings come?
Why do I want to give to support my church?

- To express gratitude to God for the blessings I have received
- To add meaning to my life and make me feel good
- To continue my family tradition of giving
- To leave a legacy
- To honor someone
- To support a special ministry in the future

Stewardship of time and talents ends at the graveside. Stewardship of treasures through "creative stewardship" continues beyond.

CHAPTER 7

Ways to Give

One basic element in creative giving is the capacity to step outside one's usual understanding to gain a new perspective and awareness. Travel in your mind's eye for a moment to a place called Galilee. Imagine yourself as one individual among a gigantic crowd that has gathered. You have brought a loved one to be healed by this man named Jesus, because you have heard that he is able to heal the lame. Further, you are deeply curious about his teachings.

This gathering place beside the water is distant from communities and desolate in appearance. Yet you and the others stay for hours, hungering for the healing touch and thirsting for the graceful word. The Teacher's close friends become alarmed and suggest that the crowd should be dismissed so that everyone might go and seek food in the villages.

When asked by Jesus, all that they can produce among themselves is five loaves and two fish, which they know to be inadequate to feed the multitude, but which they respectfully turn over to their Master. You hear the words of Jesus instructing you and the crowd to be seated on the grass, and then you see him look to heaven and bless the meager loaves. He returns them to his friends, who begin to distribute them to the eager, receptive hands. And as you see loaves appearing all around you, you realize that what had seemed insufficient has become plenty.

The miracle of the story is not really that Jesus short-circuited the process of casting seed, tending crops, harvesting and winnowing grain, grinding kernels, mixing dough, and baking loaves. The miracle is not simply Jesus bringing something into existence that moments before did not exist. The miracle is that the awareness of those who gathered was transformed. In both giving and receiving, they shared the divine blessing for which Jesus had prayed. What seemed insignificant was, indeed, mighty and plentiful. But it took "new eyes" for all to see!

When considering ways to give, it's important to begin where Jesus did—with prayer. It's the humble prayer of thanksgiving initially, and then the prayer for faithful use of all that God has provided, so that the veil that prevents us from seeing God's bounty might be lifted. It's the prayer that stumbles in the beginning because of the belief that we don't have enough to make a difference, or we feel that we need all that we have and can't spare anything significant. Our bank account just does not seem to have enough to make a difference in the larger scheme of things. But if we dare to look at all that God provides for us, then our vision begins to change, and our understanding begins to shift.

What about the cabin near the lake that you built years ago—where you took the kids for family outings? Perhaps upkeep on the property is more troublesome now that you're not going as frequently. That property may well be a small loaf that can become a creative gift.

What about the stock that you inherited from Aunt Hazel? You've never paid too much attention to its value. You've simply held on to it for sentimental reasons. Whether it has grown or diminished in value, it may still become a gift that changes lives. If it has appreciated, it may be an even more attractive gift because of the tax advantages it could provide. If it wasn't an inheritance but stock that you purchased, it might also be a valuable gift that would allow for some significant tax advantages.

Perhaps you have jewelry, fine art, or possessions that you no longer need or want. Cars, boats, motorcycles, and other vehicles can be gifted. Often they may hold more value as gifts than they might sell for. In short, almost anything of monetary value has the potential to become a gift, either outright or through a sale, which then can fund a gift.

The first decision is whether you want to have an ongoing personal financial benefit from your gift. If you do, then making a gift that can become the asset to fund a charitable gift annuity or a charitable remainder trust might be appropriate. Gift annuities usually require a gift that is either cash or easily convertible to cash. Certificates of deposit and equities (stock) make ideal gifts to fund these instruments, and they are described more fully in other chapters of this book. If it is your desire, however, to make a gift without the expectation of ongoing personal financial benefit, or if you wish to establish a trust, then other options come on the horizon. Here, assets such as real estate and other personal property may well become quite important.

Several general guidelines always need to be considered:

- The asset needs to be unencumbered. Don't expect the church or the institution to which you make the gift to pay off the balance of your debt.
- The asset needs to be easily saleable. It will not be helpful to gift recipients if they must pay property taxes, membership fees, upkeep, or other costs associated with the property.
- The asset needs to be free of any negative environmental conditions. You may, in fact, be asked to arrange and pay for an environmental study in order to assure the asset's safety and freedom from pollution.
- The value of the asset will probably need to be determined by outside professional counsel. Know ahead of time that a noncash asset could be sold at a price that is different from its appraised value, and this could have significant ramifications for your tax benefits.
- *Always* confer with appropriate legal and financial counsel before making a gift to determine the most beneficial handling, both for you and the recipient. Tax laws change, and, as a donor, you need and have a right to the most current, accurate information. This may well reduce the possibility for deleterious surprises later.
- With noncash gifts, confer with the appropriate body of the congregation or agency to ensure ahead of time that the gift will be received. This is particularly important with gifts that are deferred until a later time for actual transfer, such as a bequest through an estate.

If you are on the receiving end of a gift, whether cash or noncash, be certain that it can be managed. Even a cash gift to establish a gift annuity cannot be received, managed, and accounted for by most congregations and church agencies. They need an outside arm, such as a judicatory foundation, to undertake these responsibilities on their behalf. For noncash gifts, some general guidelines apply to the recipient as well:

- Develop specific guidelines, standards, or gift-acceptance policies *before* a gift is proposed. Be specific about all stipulations and requirements regarding matters such as appraisals and environmental reviews.
- Remember that you are representing and protecting the church or agency, and sometimes that means having to decline offers of gifts because they cannot faithfully be used as the donor wishes or as your mission requires. Proposed gifts can be declined respectfully and gracefully. Avoid jeopardizing the future of your church or institution just to please the prospective donor.
- Recognize that you are not serving your church or agency well if you move into a mode of speculation. Whatever the gift, initiate the process of selling or liquidating a noncash gift as quickly as possible.

What about hard-to-value assets? Can they be given? While some gifts may be fairly complicated to process, it may still be well worth the effort. Gifts such as commercial property, apartment buildings, and farm property may be difficult to value; however, as long as they can be appraised and sold, the income generated can provide magnificent gifts.

Other properties are even more difficult to value, such as C-corporations, S-corporations, closely held securities, and limited liability partnerships. Just because gifts such as these do not happen frequently in churches and church agencies does not mean that charitable organizations should rule out such gifts from their scopes of acceptance. It does mean, however, that receiving them will require substantial legal counsel and its associated costs, as well as the recognition that the duration of these gifts might be long-range rather than short-term.

Whether approaching the gifting process as a donor or recipient, it is clear that there is a strong spiritual component in the church and its agencies. That is why Jesus started with prayer, and so must we. Often it is through prayer as we seek guidance about what we should do with all that God provides that our eyes are opened and our understanding awakened.

Some years ago, the National Conference of Catholic Bishops released a pastoral letter on stewardship that moved beyond the usual descriptions of time, talent, and treasure. According to the pastoral letter, a good steward is one who:

- receives God's gifts gratefully;
- cherishes and tends them in a responsible and accountable manner;
- shares them in justice and love with others; and
- returns them with increase to the Lord.

If these basic tenets of Christian stewardship are clear in both head and heart, then there is no uncertainty that all that we have is God's and that we are its temporary tenders. It's clear to see, then, that there are many, many ways to give. Let us explore with our eyes and hearts open.

CHAPTER 8

Wills and Bequests

What is the greatest single change in church finances from the emergence of the new American economy? If measured simply in dollar terms, that is the easiest question raised in this book. It is a ten-digit number—$1,000,000,000. In 1992, Protestant congregations received at least $1 billion more in bequests than were received back in 1952, after allowing for inflation. In other words, after allowing for inflation, bequests to congregations have increased by a $1 billion in forty years. This does not include the value of bequests received by parachurch organizations, denominational agencies, or Christian colleges, or theological seminaries, or other Christian organizations. For the calendar year 2001, Protestant congregations in the United States received well over $3 billion in bequests. That does not include cash contributions made by living donors.[1]

When considering creative giving, one of the most basic issues is the use of a bequest in a will. While the other methods allow the possibility of tax advantages, an increased stream of income, tax benefits, and the possibility of some recognition, the starting place for many people considering creative giving is to leave something in their wills.

A bequest can be appealing for several reasons. First, the donor retains the control and benefit of his or her assets. Second, a bequest is the easiest creative giving method. Third, a bequest can be changed by a simple codicil. But making a bequest involves some challenges as well.

The first challenge is committing to writing a will. According to the *Wall Street Journal*, fewer than half of adults in the United States have wills.[2] The logical explanation is our reluctance to the idea of planning for our own deaths. This is a reality most of us simply do not want to spend time considering. We have even developed a grim sense of humor about the final distribution of our assets. Maybe you have heard some of these comments:

"How much did Bill leave when he died?"
"Well, he left it all!"

"Being of sound mind, I spent it all."

"He really didn't plan on dying so soon."

"We're spending our kids' inheritance."

"He who dies with the most toys wins."

Despite this weak attempt at coping with the reality of death in our lives, the Bible is very clear: "For we brought nothing into this world, and it is certain we can carry nothing out" (1 Timothy 6:7).

An older friend recently shared that, because of declining health, he and his wife of sixty years were planning to move from their home into an assisted-living facility. He said that he did not mind admitting that they needed some assistance, but the challenge was determining what to do with the stuff they had accumulated over the years. They had lived in the same home for thirty-five years, and there seemed to be no end to the boxes, closets, sacks, and drawers of stuff that they no longer needed.

A family member became responsible for her parents' belongings when her dad passed away and her mom experienced dementia. After two years, her parents' home was still full of stuff, despite attempts to get rid of things. And the home required continued utilities, insurance coverage, and yard maintenance.

Still another friend expressed the frustration of having to deal with his mother-in-law's possessions upon her death. After three days of sorting and distribution, no end was in sight. This is not an uncommon experience.

Recently, my sons began to express concern about the things that my wife and I have accumulated. As we discussed it, we all agreed that some things might be passed on, but there was an enormous amount of stuff that we no longer needed.

When my wife and I began to discuss this privately, however, we found that while we might not need all of the stuff, we still valued some of it. We have found it very difficult to downsize our possessions, with both of us retrieving things the other has decided to discard. Our experience illustrates the complexity and persuasiveness of the consumptive culture in which we live. And it is this culture that complicates the idea of a will.

Our experience is also an example of a theological dilemma we have. While we might say that we are stewards and that everything belongs to God, we seldom live like we really believe it. A will enables us to recognize our role as stewards and God's role as owner.

Another issue with wills is the difficulty of passing assets to rightful heirs. A well-executed or clearly written will can minimize tensions that may arise when the time comes for the distribution of assets. This issue, however, is addressed in other resources, and our purpose here is to consider wills and bequests as vehicles for creative giving.

A bequest is a simple statement in a will identifying what the donor wants to leave and to whom. A bequest can leave a percentage of liquid assets, a specific amount or item, or a more global amount—sometimes called a remainder residue—after all other obligations of the estate have been met.

Notes

1. From *The New Context for Ministry: Competing for the Charitable Dollar*, by Lyle Schaller, page 185. © 2002 Abingdon Press.
2. *The Wall Street Journal*, December 20, 2004.

BEQUEST FACTS

"Bequests are the oldest and most popular form of planned gift, constituting 80 percent of gifts."

> From "The Annual Report on Philanthropy for the Year 2004," by Giving USA, 49th Annual Issue, page 78. Researched and written at the Center on Philanthropy at Indiana University (AAFRC Trust for Philanthropy). © 2003 Giving USA.

"Of the entire population, 8 percent of adults have a charitable bequest included in a will, and 14 percent are thinking about making a charitable bequest but haven't done so yet."

> From "Giving USA Update," © 2002 Giving USA.

"Most donors have a will or estate plan. More than nine out of ten of those donors, however, have not included a church as one of the recipients of a portion of their estate."

> From *How to Increase Giving in Your Church*, by George Barna, page 33. © 1994 Regal Books.

"The median income for people with charitable bequest provisions in their wills was $60,400.00. The average age when planned gift commitment via bequest first made: forty-nine. The median bequest was $35,000.00."

> From "Giving USA Update," © 2002 Giving USA.

"Experience indicates that those organizations that consistently inform and motivate their constituency are the ones that receive the most bequest revenue."

From *Give and Take*, March 2002. © Robert F. Sharpe & Co.

"Almost half of all single females and over one-third of all single males included charitable provisions in their estate plans. In total numbers, widows and widowers constituted the largest source of charitable bequests."

From *Give and Take*, March 2001. © Robert F. Sharpe & Co.

"Our research shows that the typical bequest comes from a female who dies at about age eighty-two. She put the organization in her will at about age seventy-eight or seventy-nine, which also happens to be the age at which she stopped her regular giving."

From *Give and Take*, June 1997. © Robert F. Sharpe & Co.

"In terms of estate taxation, 91 percent of the individual bequests to charity in America are coming from estates that are not large enough to be subject to estate taxes at the levels at which they are imposed today."

From *Give and Take*, March 2001. © Robert F. Sharpe & Co.

"Most men and women who make really large bequests are small annual givers."

From *Wit, Wisdom & Moxie: A Fundraiser's Compendium of Wrinkles, Strategies, and Admonitions That Really Work*, by Jerold Panas, page 160. © 2002 Bonus Books.

"Bequest marketing also can open a dialogue with charitably motivated people who may benefit from other giving arrangements discovered through the charitable estate planning process. Bequest marketing efforts can also be an excellent way to help discover the most motivated persons among the ranks of younger donors."

From *Give and Take*, June 2001. © Robert F. Sharpe & Co.

"The number who included charity in their wills increased from 5.7 percent in 1992 to 8 percent today—40 percent growth."

From *Wit, Wisdom & Moxie: A Fundraiser's Compendium of Wrinkles, Strategies, and Admonitions That Really Work*, by Jerold Panas, page 82. © 2002 Bonus Books.

". . . [T]he average age when the first will is written is forty-four."

From *Wit, Wisdom & Moxie: A Fundraiser's Compendium of Wrinkles, Strategies, and Admonitions That Really Work*, by Jerold Panas, page 82. © 2002 Bonus Books.

"One client that enjoys a large amount of bequest income each year discovered that 25 percent of bequest donors had made average gifts of less than ten dollars during their lifetimes. Further study revealed that the average size of bequests from those persons was no less than the overall average."

From *Give and Take*, June 2003. © Robert F. Sharpe & Co.

BEQUEST QUESTIONS AND ANSWERS

Bequests are the oldest and most popular form of planned gifts. Donors like them because they are able to control and use all of their assets as long as they need them. Bequests do not immediately affect someone's lifestyle and may allow donors to make larger gifts than they ever considered before.

How are bequests made?

Bequests are directions you place in your will that explain how you want your remaining assets used.

Can I tithe my estate?

Yes. That is a type of percentage bequest.

Can I make a bequest for more than one person or charity?

Yes. There is no limit to the number of beneficiaries you may have.

Do I have to leave a specific amount or percentage?

No. That depends on your wishes, assets, and family considerations.

Are there different ways to make bequests?

Yes. The following are some of the more common methods:

- **A specific dollar amount**—assures a minimum gift size
- **A specific property**—can direct a particular item to a beneficiary
- **A percentage**—flexible as your estate changes
- **The residue**—give "what's left" after family considerations

Can I change a bequest?

Yes. A bequest can be changed at any time.

SAMPLE BEQUEST PROVISIONS

The provisions in your will for making a gift to your church or favorite charities will depend on the type of gift, as well as your own circumstances. Perhaps these model provisions will be helpful to your attorney.

The Unrestricted Gift

I give to _____First Church, a nonprofit corporation, located in Any Town, the sum of $ _____ (or _% of my estate; or the property described herein) for its general purpose.

Gift for a Specific Purpose

I give to _____First Church, a nonprofit corporation, located in Any Town, the sum of $ _____ (or _% of my estate; or the property described herein) to be used for _____(specify purpose).

Specific Legacy

I bequeath my (home, farm, livestock, car, truck, etc.,) to _____First Church, a nonprofit corporation, located in Any Town, for its general purposes.

Residuary Legatee

All the rest, residue, and remainder of my estate, both real and personal, I give to _____First Church, a nonprofit corporation, located in Any Town, for general purposes.

Memorial Fund

I give to _____First Church, a nonprofit corporation, located in Any Town, the sum of $ _____ (or _% of my estate; or the property described herein) the same to be known as "The _____ Memorial Fund," the income therefore shall be used for its general purposes (or describe the specific purpose, if desired).

Contingency Gift

I bequeath the residue of the property owned by me at my death, real and personal, and wherever situate, to my spouse, _____, if he/she survives me. If my spouse does not survive me, I devise and bequeath my residuary estate to _____First Church, a nonprofit corporation, located in Any Town, for general purposes.

Final Contingent Beneficiary

I give and bequeath the residue of the property owned by me at my death, real and personal and wherever situate, in equal shares to my above named beneficiaries, if they survive me. If my above named beneficiaries do not survive me, I give and bequeath my residuary estate to _____ First Church, a nonprofit corporation, located in Any Town, for general purposes.

Before using any of these examples, seek consultation with appropriate legal counsel.

DIRECTIONS FOR MY CELEBRATION

This worksheet includes several sets of questions. The first set helps both the pastor and the family answer questions that will be asked by the funeral home, pastor, or newspaper.

Full name: _____

Place of birth: _____

Parents' names: _____

Siblings: _____

Education:

    High school _____

    College or business school _____

    Degrees earned _____

Places of employment and positions held: _____

_____

_____

_____

_____

_____

_____

Date of retirement: _____

If married, spouse's name: _____

How did you meet your spouse? _____

_____

Date and location of marriage: _____

Children: _____

Grandchildren: _____

Great-grandchildren: _____

Have you ever received any honors or recognition? If so, what are they?

_____

_____

What civic groups have you been a part of over the years? _____

_____

_____

Positions held in civic groups: _____

_____

_____

What is your church background or history? _____

_____

Have you served as an officer, teacher, or worker in the church and, if so, in what capacity? _____

_____

The following questions are for the actual service. The answers you provide will give direction to your family and church.

What type of service do you wish to have? (Check one.)

_____ Funeral and graveside

_____ Graveside only

_____ Memorial (Please note: A memorial service means the body of the deceased is not present.)

_____ No service of any type

If you are planning to have a funeral or memorial service, where do you wish the service to be held? (Check one.)

_____ Church

_____ Funeral Home

_____ Other. Please specify where: _____

Do you wish to have a private service of family only? (Check one.)

_____ Yes   _____ No

If you are a member of a fraternal organization, do you wish for them to conduct a service? (Check one.)

_____ Yes   _____ No

If yes, the service will be held at the funeral home or graveside. Which one do you prefer? _____

Which pastor do you wish to conduct your funeral? (Check one.)

_____ The current pastor

_____ A former pastor (Name) _____

Is there any other pastor you wish to assist? (Name) _____

Music

Do you want music? (Check one.)

_____ Yes   _____ No

Before service? (Check one.)

_____ Yes   _____ No

After service? (Check one.)

_____ Yes   _____ No

Whom do you want to play the music? (Check one.)

_____ Taped music at the funeral home

_____ Funeral home organist

_____ Your church organist/pianist

Do you want the congregation to sing hymns? (Check one.)

_____ Yes _____ No

If yes, which ones: _____

Do you want a soloist to sing? (Check one.)

_____ Yes _____ No

If yes, who and what do you want them to sing? _____

_____

What type of music do you want? Give example: _____

Scriptures

Do you have a favorite Scripture(s) you want read? (Check one.)

_____ Yes _____ No

If yes, what are they? _____

_____

Do you desire to have someone other than the pastor read the Scriptures? (Check one.)

_____ Yes _____ No

If yes, who? _____

Is there someone other than the pastor you would like to talk about you? (Check one.)

_____ Yes _____ No

If yes, who? _____

Pallbearers

Whom would you like to be your pallbearers? _____
_____
_____
_____

Flowers

Do you wish to designate a memorial in lieu of flowers? (Check one.)

_____ Yes _____ No

If yes, which memorial? _____

Do you wish to give any specific instruction on flowers? (Check one.)

_____ Yes _____ No

If yes, what are your instructions? _____

_____

Other Items of Importance for You to Consider

Do you have any special wishes concerning your clothing, jewelry, etc.?

_____
_____
_____
_____

Military service _____
_____

Will you be an organ donor? (Check one.) _____

_____ Yes _____ No

Who is your attorney? _____

Where will your family find a copy of your will, funeral policies, insurance policies, and bank information? _____

Are there any special people you would like contacted at this time?
Please list:

_____

_____

_____

_____

CHAPTER 9

Instruments for Planned Gifts

The scene is an expensive restaurant. You hear the background noises of a busy, popular place for well-to-do people to meet and enjoy a delicious meal. The announcer speaks of a philanthropist who has just made a gift to the community, and you naturally assume it must be one of the well-dressed diners. Instead, the camera focuses on a smiling apron-clad waiter. The point is that anyone—even a waiter—can afford to make a planned gift. The message communicated in this commercial is that you don't have to be rich to leave a legacy.[1]

It is the same with the church. Gone are the days when cathedrals were built by the local baron. We live in the richest country the world has ever known. Today, people of all economic means throughout the church have the ability to make gifts to support the future of their faith. Planned giving offers several creative ways for donors to leave legacies by helping themselves, their families, and their favorite churches or charities.

Charitable Gift Annuities

Believed to be the oldest planned gift next to the bequest,[2] charitable gift annuities provide income and tax benefits to the donor(s) during their lifetime(s) and can then benefit selected local churches or ministries.

Several years ago, a ninety-one-year-old widow was interested in making a gift to the church that she and her husband had attended for years.

The church had been very important in their lives, and they wanted to give something back. She quickly stated that they were not millionaires and that, although they had no children, they did have heirs to whom they wanted to leave something.

The money she intended to give to the church was invested in a certificate of deposit, and she had become comfortable receiving interest from it. After conversations with her attorney, her accountant, and several heirs who were present, she determined a charitable gift annuity would help her accomplish her goals.

The day we completed the gift was an inspiring one. As the widow looked up from signing the documents, she had tears in her eyes. "You don't know how good this makes me feel," she said.

Her income would increase 167 percent. Most of the increase would be tax-free. She had a significant current income tax deduction. She even expressed glee for not having to "call around for certificate of deposit rates anymore. I hated doing that." Most touching, however, was her next statement. "You know what the best thing is?" she asked me. "Now I can give more money to my church!"

She was a tither. Since her income had increased, so would her gift to the church. People who have been generous want to continue being generous.

An annuity is simply a contract between a charity and the donor. It pays a fixed income to the donor(s) for life. The income is partially tax-free for a number of years (over the donor's life expectancy, according to Internal Revenue Service life-expectancy tables). Additionally, the donor may benefit from a current income tax deduction, an estate tax deduction, and the diversification of income-producing assets.

It doesn't take a great deal of money to create a charitable gift annuity. Forty percent of the responding charities to a 2003 American Council on Gift Annuities survey reported that they issued charitable gift annuities for $5,000.00. Fourteen percent issued charitable gift annuities for even smaller amounts.[3] You can even benefit someone else with a life income gift. It all goes back to meeting the needs and goals of the donors.

The widower was a retired engineer. His wife of fifty-plus years had passed away, but their longtime housekeeper continued to clean and cook for him several days a week. Her efforts comforted him, and the money she earned from him helped support her.

A conversation one day revealed that after his death, the housekeeper would have only a few hundred dollars a month from Social Security to live on. The widower approached us with the desire to help the woman who had been so faithful to his family, and then make a gift to his church. Using some appreciated stock to fund a charitable gift annuity, he provided an income stream to the faithful friend, received a current income tax deduction, and, after her lifetime, will be providing for his faith community with the fund the gift will establish.

A donor does not have to be elderly to create a charitable gift annuity. Twenty-eight percent of the respondents to the 2003 survey by the American Council on Gift Annuities indicated the minimum age they required was fifty-five, while an almost equal 27 percent had no minimum at all.[4]

In fact, some younger donors consider deferred-payment charitable gift annuities good methods for supplementing their retirement incomes while making charitable gifts. The gift is made now, but the payments are scheduled to begin upon retirement. Since the payment is deferred, the amount paid out is much higher than might be expected.

For example, a forty-year-old married couple funds a deferred gift annuity with $10,000.00 of appreciated stock. They choose to begin payments at retirement, or twenty-five years later. There would be a partial bypass of the gain, plus a small current income tax deduction. More dramatically, however, the payout would be 18.7 percent, or $ 1,870.00 per year for as long as either one is alive.

Charitable Remainder Trusts

Charitable remainder trusts are another form of life income gift similar to charitable gift annuities. They can be written to provide the donor(s) with income for life. A donor may use various assets to fund the trust, including cash, real estate, stocks, and bonds.

Using highly appreciated, low-income-producing assets to fund such a trust can dramatically increase income without losing a significant portion of the assets' value to capital gains tax. A current income tax deduction will be generated. After the donor's lifetime, the residual is available to support the church or ministry of the donor's choice.

Although a charitable remainder trust is similar to a charitable gift annuity, it offers more flexibility. The income may be payable as a fixed dollar amount or as a fixed percentage of the value of the trust. The payments can be made for a set number of years or for a lifetime. A donor can even receive a lifetime income and then provide income to someone else for a limited number of years, depending on several factors, including the ages of those involved.

For instance, an active church member owned some investment timberland. He regularly cut the timber, paid taxes on the gains, and invested the after-tax proceeds. He approached making a gift with three objectives in mind. First, he wished to use his timberland to make a significant gift to his church. Second, he wanted his children to inherit the land. And third, he wanted to minimize the capital gains tax on the timber sales in order to leave as much as possible to invest and generate income for him during his lifetime.

A charitable remainder trust was the perfect fit. He gave one-time cutting rights to the trust, which cut the timber and invested the total proceeds without a reduction in value for capital gains tax. Income will be sent to the donors for the rest of their lifetimes. After that, income from the trust will go to support the future of their church. And the land remains in the family.

Another flexible advantage of a charitable remainder trust is that the donor can add to it anytime after it has been established.

Wealth replacement trusts often are created simultaneously with charitable remainder trusts. Part of the income produced by the charitable remainder trust is used to purchase life insurance on the donor. The donor uses an asset that might have been inherited by a family member to fund the charitable remainder trust. Instead of receiving the asset at the time of donor's death, the heir receives the proceeds of the life insurance policy. The remaining value of the trust is then available to support the church or another organization selected by the donor. A charitable gift has been made without penalizing the heir.

A couple in their seventies was an average middle-class family. The children were grown and gone. After a career with one firm, the man retired with a pension. The woman had never worked outside the home.

Their largest investment, in the form of low-dividend stock from his previous employer, had been accumulated over thirty years through stock options at a low tax basis. They had been faithful financial supporters of their church and felt the desire to continue that after their lifetimes. They also wanted to leave as much as possible to their children. But, as people of modest means, they needed to maximize their own income during their lifetimes.

They had shared life together for over half a century. He was a cancer survivor, but she enjoyed good health.

A wealth replacement trust was a perfect fit. A gift of the highly appreciated stock into a charitable remainder trust allowed for investing the full market value of the highly appreciated stock. The 7-percent payout of the trust produced almost twice the income necessary to pay the premium on the couple's "last to die" insurance policy. The face value of the policy was equal to the current market value of the stock. The results were higher income for the couple, insurance to replace the value of the asset to the children at the donors' deaths, minimization of capital gains taxes, and a gift to their faith community.

Life Estates

A homestead is the widely recognized symbol of the American Dream. It may also be the largest asset a donor has. If the donor has no family interested in living in the home after his or her lifetime or is single with no surviving family, it may be the source of a significant gift.

A house can be given to the church through a bequest in a will. This method, however, does not give the donor an immediate tax benefit, and it may place the burden of disposal on a small or volunteer staff at the church or charity. A life estate gift can be better for both the donor and the receiving charity.

In the typical life estate arrangement, the donor deeds over the property to the church's trustees. The gift generates an immediate current income tax deduction that a bequest does not provide. If the donor pays income taxes, he or she will enjoy a financial benefit almost immediately.

The donor may continue to live in the house for as long as he or she likes, or the donor can move in with family, rent the house, and keep the rent. The donor is obligated to maintain the property for as long as he or she lives in it, uses it, or benefits from it. Upon the donor's death, the trustee sells the house and uses the proceeds to support the church or charity selected by the donor.

Always let the needs and intent of the donor guide the use of planned giving instruments. They often offer a real win-win opportunity for all involved.

Notes

1. The commercial described was prepared by Leave a Legacy, a community-based effort to help people learn about charitable giving and encourage the ordinary citizen to become a philanthropist. Leave a Legacy is organized and supported by the National Committee on Planned Giving.

2. According to a history of the Committee on Gift Annuities written by Charles Bass, who cites the belief that the first gift annuity was established in 1843.

3. The American Council on Gift Annuities, "Gift Annuity Rates Survey 2003," Question 14. *Zoomerang*. http://www.zoomerang.com/reports/public_report.zgi?ID=E3PTJJFA94CP

4. *Ibid.*, Question 11.

CHARITABLE GIFT ANNUITY QUESTIONS AND ANSWERS

A charitable gift annuity is a win-win gift. It is a way to make a gift that will ultimately benefit a charity while helping provide for donors during their lifetimes. All this and tax benefits too!

How are the rates determined?

Annuity rates are based on the age and marital status of the annuitant. In the case of a deferred annuitant, the start date of payments is a factor.

Can I create a charitable gift annuity for more than one person?

Yes. A joint-and-survivor type annuity (two-life) allows for payment to be continued for the lifetime of the survivor after the death of the first life.

How are the payments taxed?

Part of the payment is considered a return on principal and is therefore tax-free. If funded with appreciated assets, a portion of the tax-free payments will be reported as capital gains income.

Can the income beneficiary be someone other than the donor?

Yes. Payments will be made directly to the designated recipient and taxed according to his or her tax bracket, and the donor receives the deduction in the donor's bracket.

Can payments be delayed?

Yes. A deferred charitable gift annuity allows the donor to make a gift, receive a current income tax deduction, and pick a future date for payments to begin.

Can a deferred gift annuity supplement a qualified retirement plan or an IRA?

Yes. Deferred payment gift annuities can enhance retirement income.

CHAPTER 10

Creative Gifts in a Capital Stewardship Program

A capital campaign can be one of the most exciting times in the life of a church. The excitement comes from the vision painted for the future. Unfortunately, many people fear that planned gifts might take away from the main goal of encouraging immediate gifts needed for a project to get underway. It sounds risky. Is there a place for planned gifts in the capital campaign? The answer is yes!

Annual campaign support generally comes from the donor's income stream. In faith-based organizations, it is usually associated with a percentage of one's income, typically 10 percent. Generally, planned gifts are made from accumulated assets. Gifts made to a capital campaign may come from both sources, such as a portion of accumulated assets supplemented by a larger portion of the income stream for a short period of time—three to five years, for example.

Planned gifts in a capital campaign may vary in type, and they may offer the donor immediate benefits while assuring the church benefits at a later date. This aspect is acknowledged with the professional's use of descriptive terms, such as *deferred gift* or *split-interest gift*.

So how does this fit with capital campaigns?

1. Some people wish they could give now but can't until later.

These are the people who have the hearts for the gift but, for some reason, feel unsure of their ability to complete it financially. Perhaps their incomes are modest, and the assets they own are fully employed to generate whatever incomes they receive.

A life income gift might be a redeployment of assets that continues or even improves income while making a permanent, irrevocable gift to support the donor's faith. A life estate gift enables the donor to make a commitment now without losing use of the asset, which can either be lived in or rented out for future income if needed. A bequest allows the donor to enjoy the heartfelt commitment, even if he or she is unable to quantify the amount.

2. Some people can do something now and still do more later.

Some donors are capable of making gifts of a certain size now, but they have assets that would allow for larger gifts later. Perhaps they have maximized their limits on charitable deductions, but they desire to do more. Some people supporting family members with special problems will have assets to spare, but they don't know exactly when their obligations will end. Often, the sale of a business requires the founder's continued involvement, with a large final payment postponed until the successful transfer of the business. Sometimes the unexpected happens. Oil is discovered, the idea for a new invention takes root, or a garage sale bargain turns out to be a masterpiece.

3. Some people need encouragement.

In the infrequent times when a capital campaign stalls, some churches have used a matching-gift approach with planned gifts. A donor who has already made the maximum commitment to the campaign with liquid assets may be willing to make a deferred commitment if it will encourage others.

For example, the donor promises to fund a life income gift in the same amount as new donors who pledge by a specified deadline. The existing donor uses assets that are currently producing income, and he or she will continue to receive income from the planned gift. At the same time, others who have not yet made a commitment are challenged. Their gifts' values will be doubled if they act in time.

4. Some people don't like to be asked too often.

An endowment to provide funds for building maintenance and updating speaks directly to the need of a renovation capital campaign. If an endowment is in place, there might not be a need for future renovation campaigns.

5. Some people can help now before needing to pass assets on to their kids.

Charitable lead trusts are almost the opposite of typical life income gifts. They give the income to the church and leave the remainder to others, such as children. The tax deduction is based on the value of the income that is given away, rather than on the principal, as it ends up in the hands of others. It is a useful tool for estate planning with large estates. It can be particularly attractive during times of low interest rates.

6. How do you count a planned gift in a capital campaign?

You cannot count a revocable gift. Revocable means you may receive it or you may not. Even if you do, it will probably be years into the future. Never miss an opportunity, however, to allow someone to respond. Create or promote a legacy society or other recognition society. The recognition itself may help the donor fulfill the gift.

An irrevocable deferred gift, such as a charitable gift annuity or charitable remainder trust, can be counted. It will eventually mature, even though the time is usually unknown. It can be reported as a deferred gift with an approximate value.

7. How much of the campaign should be funded by deferred gifts?

While you do not want to limit the opportunity for anyone to participate, remember that these gifts tend to arrive years into the future. The project the current campaign is financing will have bills to pay in a matter of months, rather than years. Avoid the temptation to use deferred gifts with uncertain dates of maturity to make up for a shortfall in reaching your campaign goal.

8. When do we advertise the acceptance of deferred gifts?

Save creative giving opportunities for the later stages of the capital program. Your immediate needs must be addressed with immediate (or short-term) gifts. Use creative giving after eighteen months to extend gifts beyond the initial response.

9. What will be the final value of a deferred gift?

This is almost impossible to predict. The factors involved include the unknown life span of the donor and the unknown future returns on the invested assets. Valuation standards are provided by sources as diverse as the Internal Revenue Service and the National Committee on Planned Giving.

One other discussion about the value of planned gifts in a capital campaign comes from a logical thought process. If the church capital projects will require the use of a loan for immediate financing, then a deferred gift that could be applied against the loan would be helpful.

For instance, if a seventy-five-year-old donor designates a planned gift be used for a building, then, upon his or her death, the funds could be applied to debt or to deferred maintenance of the building. With age expectancy in the mid-eighties and loans ranging from fifteen to twenty years, the donor would be making a gift for the benefit of the capital projects of the campaign.

The excitement a capital campaign generates may provide the final motivation necessary to procrastinators who have been considering planned gifts. It is yet another opportunity to help people respond to the generosity of God in their lives.

CHAPTER 11

Other Issues to Consider

Initiating a planned gift requires *study*, *discussion*, and probably *counsel* with both legal and financial *professionals* in order for the decision to truly serve the well-being of both the *donors* and the *recipients*. Each of the italicized words in the preceding sentence has its own relevance in the process of considering a planned gift. Further, remember that the circumstances in which potential donors find themselves are always unique and distinctive to their particular situations.

Consideration of a planned gift is not done in a vacuum. A variety of ancillary factors must be brought to the table for examination.

Consider the role of legal and financial professionals first. Legal counsel should always be sought from an attorney who specializes in estate planning, taxation, and trusts. Likewise, seek financial consultation from certified public accountants or bookkeepers who are familiar with the donor's financial condition. If the donor intends to use invested assets for the gift, the counsel of a financial planner and/or investment professional should also be sought. While contacting all of these professionals may seem cumbersome, the contacts and counsel are essential to the formation of a planned gift that serves both the donor and the recipient.

What if you, as a prospective donor, do not have an attorney who specializes in estate planning and the tax laws associated with philanthropic gifts and gift instruments? How do you find an attorney? While the Yellow

Pages are one source of information, the extent of current information is much greater on the Internet. (Addendum 11-A provides some guidelines for researching and locating qualified attorneys.)

Three of the key issues with which your attorney can assist are the development of a current will, a durable power of attorney, and a living will, or advance medical directive. All three of these instruments are critical to a comprehensive estate plan. The current will allows for you to describe how you want your assets to be managed following your death. When a person dies without a will, he or she is said to die intestate, and state laws determine how the possessions and other assets of the deceased are to be passed along to others. Such a distribution does not allow for charitable gifts, regardless of the activity and commitment to a church, educational institution, or social service agency that an individual might have had while living. Your attorney will be helpful in interpreting state laws that affect the specific planning of your will.

Preparation of a durable power of attorney is also essential. This legal instrument authorizes the person you designate to act on your behalf and conduct your personal and/or professional business if you become unable or incompetent to manage your affairs. It is written with specific guidelines and limitations according to your circumstances and desires. Both a will and a durable power of attorney can be changed at a later time if conditions or preferences change.

In the spring of 2005, the barrage of stories in virtually every news and information medium focused on the extremely complicated and heart-wrenching story of Terri Schiavo, a woman who had been left in a condition termed by her doctors as a persistent vegetative state. At issue was the whether to continue the nutrition provided to Ms. Schiavo through a feeding tube.

Ms. Schiavo's story illustrates the importance of having another legal document in your estate plan. Prepared with the assistance of your attorney and shared with your family and doctors, the advance medical directive, or living will, describes your preferences for administering or, especially, withdrawing or withholding life-sustaining medical treatment, including nutrition and hydration, in the event of terminal illness, permanent unconsciousness, or irreversible mental incompetence.

What has been clear in the case of Ms. Schiavo is the emotional pain experienced by her family members, who disagreed about the steps to be taken. An advance medical directive would have defined those steps more specifically, honored the patient's wishes, and relieved her loved ones of having to make decisions without her guidance.

Families with children—particularly those with minor children—have additional issues that they must consider in their estate plans. It is through a will or a living trust that declarations can be made about the care of minor children until they reach maturity.

Since the will is a legally constructed, binding document, it needs to be kept current. Updating it as conditions change is one of parents' most important responsibilities. The will, or even a living trust, however, is not meant to convey all parental wishes in detail.

A second document, known as a Letter of Intent, may accompany the will. This letter is not a legal document, but in it, parents may describe their children's background and their hopes for their children's future. It too requires updating as children mature, and older children can help prepare the letter to better represent their interests. The letter is kept current and ready for those who will assume guardianship or care for the children should the parent or guardian pass away or become incapacitated.

A third document, the Ethical Will, allows parents to share values, life lessons, hopes, and dreams, as well as love and forgiveness with family and community. This nonlegal will is a legacy that has little or nothing to do with money, except, perhaps, teachings about beliefs in the importance of Christian stewardship. From its ancient Jewish origins, it has always been a window to the soul of the deceased, and it becomes a farewell message of deeply felt emotions and personal philosophies to those closest to the departed.

Another document that is important for persons of all ages, regardless of responsibilities for care of children, is a Letter of Instruction. This letter states what should happen after an individual's death, including contact information for death notifications, funeral instructions, obituary information, asset and debt explanations, and locations of important paper documents. This letter can spell out the wishes regarding organ donation, autopsy, management of the body, and care of pets and other special property. It can also be recorded electronically as a videotape, audiotape, or compact disc and made available to loved ones, but a full transcript should also be maintained. (Addendum 8-D provides a guide for creating this document.)

For millions of Americans, the linchpin of financial stability during retirement is the benefits they receive from Social Security. Their financial well-being is largely connected to the regular income they receive as a result of years of income-producing work. Closely related to this are the healthcare benefits they receive through Medicare. For others, Social Security serves more as a source of discretionary income that allows for travel, optional purchases, and charitable giving.

One of the planning issues that couples receiving Social Security must consider is the probable reduction in income when one of the two dies. The surviving spouse may be forced to contend with significant reductions at that time. An ethical issue in estate planning, therefore, is to maintain a farsighted perspective that assures that any gift made does not endanger the capacity of one or both of the donors to be satisfactorily cared for during their eldest years. This is another point where professional counsel can be employed to develop meaningful projections for financial needs during the later years of life.

While the Social Security Administration cannot give guidance about the appropriateness of planned gifts, it can provide both general and specific information to assist in overall financial planning for later years. Broad, current, and accurate information is available through the official website of the U.S. Social Security Administration, Social Security Online, at www.ssa.gov. The site also provides extensive related information through links to various sites ranging from regional services provided within or near a particular ZIP Code, to concerns related to veterans' services, tax preparation assistance, legislative issues, and various methods of contacting the Social Security Administration for direct assistance.

As life spans extend, so do the number of people who describe themselves as part of the "Sandwich Generation." These individuals and couples discover that, even in retirement years, they are responsible for the care and support of their aging parents, as well as a younger generation (or two) seeking to achieve academic goals or beginning the process of establishing their professional lives while starting families of their own.

Along with this spread of responsibilities comes the necessity of those in the Sandwich Generation to consider the most effective deployment of financial resources for aging parents, particularly when they can no longer attend to those responsibilities themselves; to honor the values and intentions of those aging parents; and to assure their physical, social, mental, and spiritual well-being as their dependency on others grows. For generations that are just beginning, planned gifts with deferred benefits can help meet the costs of higher education when the time comes. Here again, the counsel of professional financial planners, as well as the services of professional gift planners, can be of inestimable value to assure that any decisions made provide the most benefit to the donors and to the recipients.

Oh yes, the recipients! It is easy for a donor to believe that a recipient will be as thrilled to receive a gift as the donor is in making it. Some of the issues around special gifts are considered in other chapters of this book. One matter that donors need to consider here, however, is how he/she/they want the gift to be used; how they want it to benefit the church, institution, or agency to which they're making the gift; and whether they ever want the principal of the gift to be touched. More than one argument has emerged following receipt of a gift, which gives evidence to the fact that differences between a recipient's understanding and a donor's intent can arise. Writing instructions about an intended or eventual gift using one of the documents described earlier in this chapter can help avoid such misunderstandings.

ADDENDUM 11-A

GUIDELINES FOR SELECTING AN ATTORNEY

The consideration of planned gifts is a deeply personal matter. It evolves from some of our most significant personal values and focuses on some of the most confidential matters of spiritual, financial, philanthropic, and familial well-being. Therefore, securing legal counsel with whom we are comfortable and confident is essential.

The World Wide Web is a dynamic source of information, with new sites added often, revisions and expansions constantly made to existing information, and addresses altered with great frequency. It is a source that merits time and effort in the discovery and decision-making process of selecting legal counsel, and it can provide far more comprehensive information than the Yellow Pages or "just asking around." The sites identified here are current at the time of this writing, and by the time of reading there will, in all probability, be additional sources available.

www.abanet.org

The American Bar Association's public website provides general information about estate planning and selected components of an estate plan, including an introduction to wills, an explanation of the probate process, and descriptions of the legal ramifications of specific options for consideration in estate planning.

www.lawyers.com

This site has a page entitled "Trusts and Estates: Selecting a Good Lawyer." It acknowledges that "there are some attorneys who hold themselves out as experts in trusts and estates, but who have little or no experience in this area of practice."[1] It then proceeds to provide over a dozen steps that may be taken to review attorneys' backgrounds and identify areas of expertise.

The site also provides pages that focus on preparing for and meeting with a lawyer when engaged in estate planning and considering gift possibilities. Web pages describe various instruments to include in a personal estate plan and provide a search engine for looking up definitions of legal terms. Another resource enables the user to search for information by attorney name.

www.actec.org

The American College of Trust and Estate Counsel website provides a toolbox to assist with information; calculators of various kinds for IRAs, tax, and amortization; ethics; Internal Revenue Service resources and forms; and other diverse and relevant topics. Also included are listings of their fellows by city and state.

State Bar Associations

Each of these organizations' websites provides various public services and resources, with links to companion sources of information, organizations, and listings.

It should be noted that all of these sites and links are for the purpose of providing public information only and are not intended to provide legal advice. This can occur only when an individual officially retains or engages an attorney or firm for the purpose of receiving specific legal counsel in the selected area of expertise.

Note

1. *LexisNexis Martindale-Hubbell Lawyers.com.* © 2004 Martindale-Hubbell.

CHAPTER 12

When, Where, and How

The people of the United States are arguably some of the wealthiest and most generous people in the world. According to Giving USA 2004, in 2003, total giving reached an estimated $240.72 billion, 74.5 percent of which came from individuals. Approximately 35.9 percent of the total, or $86.39 billion, was given to religious organizations.[1] We are a generous people, especially to our faith.

> For Christians, there is an especially attractive universality about planned giving, in that almost everyone is capable of participating. Everyone, rich or poor, will create an estate during his or her lifetime. When we have embraced stewardship as a lifelong Christian value, planned giving provides a welcome opportunity to ensure that the Church and those charities which have been important throughout our life also figure in our estate planning.[2]

If we have done the financial analysis explained in Chapter 6, we know our people have the financial ability to make planned gifts to support their faith.

When?

The answer is now. All of us are constantly bombarded with financial information. Many television networks and radio talk shows focus on how we should earn and spend our money. This is all done in the form of education.

Usually, a local church needs to establish a permanent fund or an endowment committee. One of the responsibilities given to the committee is to receive and administer the bequests, trusts, and trust funds generally associated with endowment or permanent funds.

Once a committee has been established, the members need to be chosen carefully. Who should they be? Don't make the common error of assuming that those who appear affluent or have careers in related fields will make the best members. Instead, choose people who have demonstrated their hearts for the church with histories of loyal giving. Look for those who are not afraid to express their beliefs. Naturally, they should be the ones who are listened to when they speak.

Committee members need to be educated about the possibilities and advantages of planned gifts. They do not need to know how to draft a trust or calculate percentages. They do need to understand that planned giving can help a donor achieve his or her own goals.

Do not be surprised when they become early donors of your planned giving effort. In fact, expect it. How could they more earnestly recommend the concept of planned giving than by saying, "I tried it. I liked it."?

One church developed a "Declaration of Intent." (A sample is provided in Addendum 12-A.) Can you imagine how encouraging it would be for a committee to tell the congregation that all of its members had made or were in the process of making planned gifts to support the church ministries?

Where?

What safer place is there for people to learn than the hallowed ground of their church? And how do people learn? Some people learn through the written word, so a prominent display of brochures in a common area of the church works well. Keep it well stocked with current material.

We have all heard of the benefits of repetition in education. Articles telling how individuals and families benefited from making planned gifts should appear regularly in the church's newsletter. One-liners and/or thought-provoking questions can be printed in bulletins. Some people advocate adding a request that the church be remembered in wills to any piece of written material disseminated by the church.

Some of us learn best at workshops and seminars. These can be offered on church property or off, but they should be sponsored by the church.

It is important that the presenter be a capable speaker who understands that it is not a forum for selling products. The basic ideas can be presented in an hour.

How?

It begins with the church leadership. Both the clergy and lay leaders must understand the benefits of planned giving. If this is such a good idea, shouldn't the pastor preach about it? How about a sermon on the gifts mentioned in the Bible? How about references to gifts that have already affected the lives of those sitting in the pews?

In the seventh chapter of his book, *Creating a Climate for Giving*, Don Joiner describes a five-year planned giving promotional plan.[3] It begins with educating the leadership and asking for their participation. It utilizes both the ideas described above and others. It is simple and easy to follow. Adopt a plan of action, and follow through. It is a year-round effort that should be continued year after year. If a planned giving program is really going to be effective, then consistency is required.

People will want to know why the church is telling them about planned giving. They'll want to know they can trust the church to use its resources wisely. Adopt a gift-acceptance policy to increase interest, build trust, and assist both donors and the church in communicating and planning effectively.

Help people see the vision. Translate what their gifts can do. What areas in particular warrant assistance? Could it be scholarships for seminary students? Perhaps a historic sanctuary is taking increasing amounts of money to maintain. A mission trip may have touched the hearts of some people who would like others to experience the joy of helping those who are less fortunate.

Use your imagination. Remember, we are addressing the need of the giver to give. If the church is enabled to continue to minister to the people of the community, are we not supporting the great commission?

Notes

1. Giving USA 2004, 94.

2. From *The Passionate Steward: Recovering Christian Stewardship from Secular Fundraising*, by Michael O'Hurley-Pitts, page 153. © 2001 St. Brigid Press.

3. Joiner, 92–94.

DECLARATION OF INTENT

It is with deep satisfaction that I declare my intent to support our faith in future generations and assure the ministry and Christian service of the

First Church
Anytown

Therefore . . .

_____ I have provided for the support of my church through a:

_____ bequest in my will

_____ planned gift

_____ life insurance beneficiary designation

_____ retirement plan beneficiary designation

_____ I will provide for the support of my church or _____ by a bequest in my will in the next _____ months.

_____ I would like to benefit both my family and my church through a life income gift.

_____ I would like to give my house to support my church after my lifetime.

I understand this Declaration of Intent is not a legal obligation and may be changed at my discretion.

_____

Name (printed)

_____

Signature   Date

You may use my name if it will be helpful in encouraging others to provide for the future of the faith.
Yes _____ No _____

CREATIVE GIVING WORKSHOP OUTLINE

I. Opening
    A. Welcome/introductions
    B. Prayer
    C. Purpose of workshop

II. Faith and Finance Facts
    A. America's wealth/concerns
    B. Spiritual issue/denominational tradition
    C. Trends

III. Do We Really Need a Will?
    A. Why we don't make wills
    B. How to make a will that works
    C. What a will can and cannot do
    D. What does a will cost?
    E. Can my will be changed?
    F. How often should it be reviewed?
    G. What about estate taxes?
    H. How can I remember the church in my will?

IV. Creative Giving
    A. Wills and bequests
    B. Charitable gift annuities
    C. Charitable remainder trusts

V. What Difference Can I Make?

VI. Closing
    A. Thanks to all
    B. Resources/private, no-cost consultation available
    C. Declaration of Intent
    D. Evaluation form
    E. Prayer

CREATIVE GIVING WISH LIST

Does a particular ministry of your church warm your heart? Perhaps you have been supporting it since it began, and you have seen the good it has done. You want it to continue into the future.

Creative giving may provide the way. In fact, it may allow you to give a far more substantial gift than you ever thought you could. The endowment fund you dedicate to that special ministry can make sure it continues to:

- provide scholarships for those seeking a seminary education;
- maintain the beautiful building where you worship;
- support a children's home;
- maintain the church cemetery;
- provide scholarships for youth attending mission trips;
- help support ministerial pensions;
- provide missionary support;
- support the food pantry operated out of the church;
- help construct a new building;
- provide flowers on a particular date to mark the life of a loved one;
- promote children's ministries;
- provide scholarships for children of your church to attend college;
- provide attractive retreat facilities;
- support elderly housing and nursing care;
- provide housing for retired pastors and their spouses;
- help with the upkeep of camps and retreat centers;
- pay for school supplies for a community center; and/or
- fund the minister's emergency fund.

CHAPTER 13

Church Decisions

Initiating and maintaining a creative giving program in any congregation, regardless of its size, is a process that requires time, energy, thoughtfulness, vision, commitment, and a lot of prayer. It requires considerable patience as well, because multiple steps need to be taken in order for the program to be successful and enduring. Enthusiasm about getting a program started can diminish the effectiveness of the program if steps are skipped or decisions by appropriate church bodies are omitted. Deliberateness and systematic attention are key, both in the beginning and along the path of expanding a creative giving program. Just as a congregation would not hastily and without due diligence buy a piece of real estate, start a new worship service, begin a day school, or add to or reduce its staff without close analysis and clarity of vision, so must there be intentional analysis and planning from the beginning (or restoration) of a creative giving program.

The beginning point is clarity of purpose. The basis of that clarity must be a theologically sound understanding. If the intent is simply to get money for the church before the older generation dies off, then the program is on a slippery slope from its beginning. Church members will quickly spy such a shabby purpose.

The biblical, theological, and philosophical grounding has been addressed in Chapter 3 of this book and in the companion book, *Faith and*

Money.[1] Begin with the recognition that all that we have comes from and belongs to God. It is provided as an expression of God's love for our well-being and as an impetus to do God's work in the world.

What is critical here is that this is not simply a mental construct; it is a conviction of heart. The initiation of a creative giving program provides a unique opportunity for the congregation to learn about the biblical footing and the application of biblical principles in our lives. Just as with the offering on Sunday morning, we give because it is essential to the faithful expression of our gratitude to God and to our discipleship. The purpose, then, of the biblically grounded and theologically sound creative giving program is to provide structure and protection for the gifts that are made in gratitude and trust of the long-term effectiveness of the church's ministry.

With this conviction in mind and heart, the beginning point for action is probably within the congregation's officially designated finance committee. It may be that the committee's common driving force is one of need for additional income for the church coffers, because the committee is responsible for planning and overseeing church finances. What a splendid moment, though, for biblical teaching and prayerful discernment!

The committee's recommendations to the church's official governing board should outline and describe the steps necessary to develop a comprehensive creative giving program. These recommendations will provide for some candid dialog about the nature and meaning of faithful living—and, perhaps, about the nature and meaning of the church as well.

Once the recommendations have been prepared and approved by the finance committee, the dialog shifts to the church's governing body. The recommendations should not simply be that the church have a creative giving program, but rather that the biblical, theological, and practical relevance for such a program be considered by a relatively small, broad-based task group and that a recommendation be returned within a given time frame. Further, if the task group finds that the formation or reactivation of a creative giving program is appropriate and timely, then the group should develop a charter outlining such matters as the role and function of the program, how its assets will be managed, the makeup and accountability of the overseeing committee, the scope of its responsibility, and its interdependence with other church bodies. (A sample charter is attached as Addendum 13-A.)

Included in the charter should be an outline of how members of the creative giving committee are to be nominated and elected, the length of their terms, and a maximum number of consecutive years of eligibility to serve. Usually a rotation system serves most effectively to strengthen continuity and assure the flexibility of having new members bring new perspectives, energy, and networks to the congregation. No committee should be dominated by a single individual or group, so tenures should be specified.

To strengthen the accountability to the full congregation through its governing body, it is preferable to use the same system of nominating and electing members that is used with other groups in the congregation. The task group might also be charged with the responsibility of drafting a gift-acceptance policy if one has not already been developed, approved, and interpreted to the congregation. (A sample gift-acceptance policy is attached as Addendum 13-B.) All of the material and recommendations would be processed through the finance committee and then brought back to the church's governing body for final action.

Remember the myths described in Chapter 2? Through this process of discussion and decision by several groups, many of these myths can be addressed in a straightforward manner and debunked before they become troublesome to the planning process.

While these steps may seem overly cumbersome, they are important for several reasons. The first is to build the group of church members and officials who are being exposed to the meaning, relevance, and importance of having a comprehensive creative giving program. Second, each time the members of another group become familiar with the concept and meaning of a creative giving program, the "ownership" of the program is broadened and enhanced. A creative giving program will seldom be successful if it is seen as "their" program. Third, the steps initiate a process of building essential trust. The program's success will be highly dependent on the trust that church members have in the program, its leaders, and the sense that assets given to the church will be well managed and used in accordance with the donor's values, desires, and preferences.

One of the key elements in the flow of these decisions is the basic intentionality at each step along the way. Each church official—whether a member of the finance committee, the governing board, or the task group named to analyze the need for and potential of the congregation in having a creative giving program—must realize the long-term implications of forming or revitalizing such a program. Creating a program, only to abandon it in a year or five years—either by official action or neglect—destroys the likelihood that the congregation will be able to develop a similar program for another decade or more. Abandoning a creative giving program registers in the hearts and minds of the congregation that such discipleship is not important. This false, heretical teaching, whether intended or not, will be difficult to overcome in the future because of the insidious nature of persistent doubt.

Four matters merit the special attention of the task group developing the operational charter for the creative giving program. The first is to develop a policy regarding the acceptance, management, and application of memorial gifts. For a congregation that does not already have an active memorial program, the decision to establish one is timely in connection with the development of a comprehensive planned giving program. Although it is not new, the trend of suggesting alternatives to flowers as commemorative remembrances and expressions of condolence is prevalent and appropriate. Even the most avid flower lover would not choose a wasteful, short-lived floral arrangement over gratefully given cash to a fund that had meaning to the deceased. The irony is that even though most church members want their pastor to conduct the funeral or memorial service, and perhaps have the service in their church, newspaper obituaries belie the failure of churches to encourage memorial gifts to the church to perpetuate the loving presence of the deceased.

If a memorial fund already exists, then enveloping existing monies into a memorial endowment or endowments will provide the perpetuity of memory that many families prefer. If a memorial committee already exists, then coalescing the involvement of that group with the work of a newly formed creative giving committee will be essential to avoid conflicting activities and hurt feelings once the new committee is fully functioning. If a memorial committee is well ensconced in the life of the congregation, then it may continue to serve very effectively in tandem with the new committee. Formation of the latter does not require abandonment of former. It does, however, necessitate some new guidelines of responsibility and cooperation.

Another matter to be addressed by the task group is how undesignated bequests will be handled and into whose responsibility they will fall. For instance, if Mr. Beloved leaves a $15,000.00 bequest to First Church, who has the authority to receive and manage the gift? Some denominations assign this responsibility to a specific group in the congregation. Or, that group may assign the responsibility to another group, such as the newly formed or reactivated creative giving committee.

Unless it is specified otherwise in their bequests, donors of estate funds ordinarily prefer that their bequests be of long-term benefit to the congregation, rather than be consumed in the short term. The endowment is the more appropriate recipient of a bequest than the momentary needs of the building and grounds committee or the emergency drive to erase the preschool debt.

The urgency to have this matter of authority clarified in advance is amplified if Mr. Beloved's bequest is real or personal property, rather than cash. There are many more issues to be resolved in the decision to receive and manage the bequest of such property. A general guideline, however, is for the new creative giving committee to be responsible for submitting a recommendation to the church's governing body regarding the acceptance of the property and, if the action is to receive it, then the new committee assumes responsibility for managing undesignated bequests to the church.

Third, the task group charged with developing guidelines for the new creative giving program should also consider the initial formation of three separate endowments—a general endowment fund, a capital endowment fund, and an endowment fund for missions and outreach ministries. These endowments could begin with funds from individual gifts, memorial gifts, regular modest allocations from the church's operating budget, special fundraising events and offerings, "adoption" by various groups in the church, and other means that the task group might develop.

In the beginning, the important issue is clarity about the diversity of funds to benefit various parts of the church ministry. Additional endowment funds may be established to support such programs as music, children's, and youth ministries. An essential understanding is that these are complementary funds, rather than competitive funds. By complementing each other and supplementing the regular giving of members and friends of the congregation, distributions from the endowment funds tend to expand, rather than diminish, ministry opportunities.

A fourth issue to be addressed by the task group is to provide a clear statement that the endowment is to support the church ministry. It is not simply the role of the new creative giving committee to *grow* the endowment for the sake of having a larger endowment at the end of the year. The role of the committee is to manage the endowments for growth *and for support* of the ministries in the fulfillment of the church's God-given calling. A committee hoarding resources is no more faithful than an individual doing the same, no matter how righteous the intent may seem. Endowments come into being because of generosity, and these endowments must demonstrate generosity in turn. Endowments are a means to an end—faithful ministry—and never an end unto themselves.

What begins with the action of the church finance committee moves through the governing council that establishes a task group to consider the role of a creative giving program in the church. The work of the task group sets the scene for the effective ministry of the new program. Their recommendations move back to the finance committee and other affected groups in the church, and then to the governing council.

Deliberations of the possibilities will be many, but when these are consistently set within the practice of prayer and open communication, the decisions that emerge have the potential to lead the church to new, stronger ministries, thanks to expanding financial support. What more could one want from a succession of meetings, conversations, prayers, and decisions?

Note

1. Reeves and Tyler, *Faith and Money*.

CHARTER

(LEGAL NAME) CHURCH
(CITY) (STATE)
THE ENDOWMENT PROGRAM

THE PURPOSE

The Endowment Program of (NAME) Church, located in (CITY), (STATE), hereafter referred to in this document as "the Endowment Program," is established for the purpose of providing members and friends opportunities to make charitable gifts to (NAME) Church that will become a permanent endowment of financial support and a living memorial. The Endowment Program is intended for purposes that are not a part of the church's established programs that are funded through the annual operating budget of the church and the regular giving of its members.

ADMINISTRATION

The Endowment Program shall be administered by the Permanent Endowment Fund Committee of (NAME) Church, hereinafter referred to as the "Committee," under authority granted by the church's governing board. The Committee shall have no fewer than five (5) members and no more than nine (9) members. The members of the Committee shall be nominated by the church's official nominating body and elected by the church's governing board and shall serve three-year terms. Three classes with terms ending in consecutive years shall provide a system of rotation of members. Members may be reelected but shall not serve more than twelve (12) consecutive years.

During its first meeting of each calendar year, the Committee shall elect a President, Vice President, Secretary, and Treasurer to serve the responsibilities ordinarily assigned to those positions and such other officers and subcommittees as it deems necessary. The Secretary shall be charged with the responsibility of the collection and safekeeping of documents associated with the conduct of business of the Endowment Committee. The Treasurer shall assure a thoroughness of record that retains clear information regarding the source and particulars of all funds.

The Committee shall cooperate with such other bodies of the church as necessary to assure that an annual audit is conducted, which shall include all assets under the control and auspices of the Committee.

The Committee shall make a full report no less frequently than once each year to the church's governing board and shall be perpetually accountable to that governing board.

INVESTMENT OF ENDOWMENT FUNDS

The Endowment Program's investment objectives are:

1. Conservation of principal for the effective maintenance of purchasing power;
2. Regular income at a reasonable rate;
3. Growth of income and principal over and above that necessary to offset cost-of-living increases; and
4. Investment of assets in institutions, companies, corporations, or funds that make a positive contribution toward the maintenance of established principles of the denomination.

All gifts received by the Endowment Program shall be invested through the establishment of one or more accounts with a denominational or commercial organization duly qualified to manage, grow, and regularly report on the status of the investment(s). Decisions regarding specific investments shall be made by one or more professional consultants paid for such counsel. It shall be preferred that non-members of the (NAME) Church shall serve in this capacity. The placement of all investments shall be by the approval of a majority of the members of the Committee, and no member of the Committee shall inure personal financial gain from the investment practices and procedures of the Endowment Program. Invested funds may be transferred to another investment institution with the approval of a majority of the members of the Committee. The specific purpose of each account authorized by the Committee shall be stated in order to fulfill the wishes of the donor and thereby to segregate and maintain gifts for their stated purposes.

LIMITATION ON USE OF PRINCIPAL

The objectives of the Endowment Program are to conserve principal and make use of only the distributions determined by the Committee. Any part of the principal may be withdrawn only in extreme and overwhelming circumstances, bordering on the survival of (NAME) Church. Any withdrawal of principal must be approved by a two-thirds (2/3) vote of the church's governing board at which a quorum is present.

DISTRIBUTIONS FROM THE ENDOWMENT PROGRAM

Distributions from accounts in the Endowment Program shall be taken by the Committee as directed by the donors at the time of their gifts or as directed by wills or other gift documents if such direction is in conformity with the general purposes set forth herein. In the case of undesignated gift accounts, the amount of all distributions shall be determined by the Committee that shall keep in mind the Endowment Program investment objectives stated above in this document. The purposes and causes to which distributions from undesignated gift accounts are to be made shall be approved by a majority of the members of the Committee. All distributions shall be reported to the church's governing board at its next meeting.

GIFTS TO THE FUND

Gifts to the Endowment Program shall be classified as "designated" or "undesignated" and then assigned to one of the following categories:

A. Mission Funds (for missions in and beyond the local church and community);

B. Property Funds (for maintenance, care, improvements or additions to, or construction of physical facilities);

C. General Endowment Funds (for special needs and ministries determined by the church leadership); or

D. A specified ministry area designated by a donor, *e.g.*, the music ministry of the church or new programs serving children in the neighborhood, etc. (This could be included in the General Endowment if bookkeeping practices permit it.)

The Committee shall have the authority and responsibility to accept or decline any and all gifts to the Endowment Program in keeping with the authority granted by the church's governing board and in keeping with the Gift-Acceptance Policy adopted by the church's governing board.

The Committee may receive and manage at its discretion assets that are not considered permanent assets of the church, such as a facilities reserve fund or operations reserve fund.

(NOTE: For administrative reasons, consideration might be given to the establishment of a standard minimum amount when a gift is designated to create a new or separate permanent endowment fund. Consideration might also be given to allowing a specific time period in which such an endowment might reach a preset minimum amount. If the endowment does not reach that goal by the stated time period, then provisions can be made for (1) transfer of the gifts to a General Endowment, or (2) the endowment not to make any distributions until the corpus reaches a certain amount. Once a designated permanent endowment has been created, gifts of any size can be accepted. If such a policy is desired, it should be incorporated in this document.)

Memorial gifts received by the Endowment Program shall be considered permanent assets of the Program and, following consultation with immediate family members of the deceased, may be added to an existing fund or placed in a new fund. At the discretion of the Endowment Committee, a Memorial Fund may be established to receive all memorial gifts not placed in other named funds. Management of the asset and decisions about distributions shall rest with the Endowment Committee, subject to the concurrence of the church's governing board.

All provisions of the Endowment Program as to investment of funds, administration of funds, and limitation of use of distributions shall be applicable to both designated and undesignated gifts, and all gifts made to the Fund shall be accepted subject to the terms and limitations set forth in this document.

MANAGEMENT OF BEQUESTS

By action of the church's governing board on (DATE), all bequests, unless designated by the donor to be directed elsewhere, shall be directed to the Endowment Program and shall become the responsibility of the Endowment Committee for management and oversight. The Endowment Committee shall also hold the responsibility of maintaining communication with family members of benefactors, donors, and others as deemed appropriate.

LIABILITY OF MEMBERS OF THE COMMITTEE

In the absence of gross negligence or fraud, no member of the Endowment Committee or other church body responsible for the management of the assets under the auspices of the Committee shall be personally liable for any action or omission made with respect to the Endowment Program.

MERGER, CONSOLIDATION, OR DISSOLUTION OF (NAME) CHURCH

If at any time (NAME) Church is lawfully merged or consolidated with any other church, all the provisions declared in this Charter in respect to the Endowment Program shall be deemed to have been made on behalf of the merged or consolidated church, which shall be authorized to administer the same in all respects and in accordance with the terms thereto. If (NAME) Church should ever be dissolved without any lawful successor thereto, the Fund, including principal and realized and unrealized gains to date, shall....

(*NOTE: At this point in the document, direction should be given as to disposition of the Endowment Program assets in the event the local church is dissolved. Ideas might include:*

(a) *Entrusting a denominational foundation with making distributions while maintaining the principal as an endowment; or*
(b) *Directing the distribution of principal and accumulated income to one or more denominational institutions.*)

AMENDMENTS

Technical corrections and amendments to the Endowment Program which do not alter the stated purpose of the Endowment Program may be made by a two-thirds (2/3) affirmative vote at a duly called governing board of (NAME) Church at which a quorum is present.

SEVERABILITY

If any provisions or any application of any provisions of the Endowment Program shall be held or deemed to be or shall be illegal, inoperative, or unenforceable, the same shall not affect any other provisions or any application of any provisions herein contained or render the same invalid, inoperative, or unenforceable.

This Endowment Program Charter was adopted this _____ day of
_____, 20____ in a duly authorized _____
(IDENTIFY THE CHURCH'S GOVERNING BOARD) of (NAME)
Church, (CITY), (STATE), by a vote of ____ For, _____ Against, and _____
Abstained.

_____
Recording Secretary

_____
Denominational Official

_____
Pastor

*This document has been substantially adapted from a similar charter
prepared by a committee of planned giving professionals associated with the
National Association of United Methodist Foundations. That organization
bears no responsibility for the content of this adaptation. Each local
church developing its endowment program may adapt the document further to make it applicable to its particular situation, e.g., by employing
denominational nomenclature for the governing body. Legal counsel is recommended to assure final concurrence with applicable state and local
statutes and laws.

SAMPLE GIFT-ACCEPTANCE POLICIES

Please review and revise these policies as needed. An attorney and/or real estate agent should review the terminology and basic recommendations.

1. Unrestricted cash gifts will be accepted and acknowledged through the normal accounting procedures of _____ First Church.

2. Designated gifts will be accepted for approved memorials and tributes only. These opportunities are:

   _____

   These opportunities are available for memorials or tributes on a basis of first response through the chairperson of the _____ Committee. The committee has absolute responsibility for accepting memorials and tributes and establishing appropriate recognition procedures.

3. Receipt of noncash gifts will be the responsibility of the _____ Committee. The Committee reserves the right to decline or return any gift determined to be unacceptable due to value, marketability, environmental concerns, or any other reason deemed problematic to the _____ First Church.

4. All noncash gifts (except for real estate) will be immediately liquidated by the _____ Committee. Gifts of stock, various kinds of securities, insurance products, automobiles, animals, jewelry, and other items of value must be unencumbered and given outright to _____ First Church. If the gift is deemed acceptable to the committee, then the gift will immediately be sold in a manner deemed most appropriate by the Committee.

5. All gifts of real estate must be given with an appropriate title search, environmental evaluation, survey, and appraisal. All costs of transferring

will be born by the donor. Gifts of real estate must also be unencum-bered by liens, litigation, or any other potential liability for _____ First Church. Before title is accepted by_____ First Church, the _____ Committee reserves the right not to accept the gift.

6. All noncash gifts will be acknowledged in a dated letter from the Chairperson of the _____ Committee that will include a description of the gift. There will be no appraisal, acknowledgement of appraisal, or determination of value offered in the acknowledgment process. The donor has sole responsibility to the Internal Revenue Service for identifying the value of any noncash gift.

7. Any questions regarding this policy should be referred to the Chairperson of the _____ Committee.

CHAPTER 14

Leadership Roles

The telephone rings, and the conversation begins.

"John, this is Pastor Ed. I have a very important matter I want to talk to you about. Do you have a few minutes?"

"Of course, Pastor . . . unless you want me to preach for you Sunday. That might take longer than a few minutes." *[They chuckle together.]*

"No, that's not my agenda right now. Good idea, though. I'll just keep that in mind until planning gets underway for our next Laity Sunday. *[They chuckle again.]*

"What I'm calling about is the new endowment committee that the board approved last week. You know, I was really impressed with the way the task group had researched the whole issue of creative giving and brought a thorough report back with their recommendation that we begin a creative giving program as soon as possible. You were there, and you know that we talked about it for quite a while before the board approved it unanimously.

"As I've thought about it, there didn't seem to be anyone who was ever against the recommendation. There were just a good many questions that were raised, and our friend Gloria did a great job of responding to them. What did you think about the discussion?"

"Oh, I thought it was one of the best discussions our board has had in a long time. Of course, it helped to have such a well-prepared presentation by Gloria and the task group. You may not remember, Pastor, but when you were new here, I mentioned that I hoped you'd push us to get an endowment program started."

"I remember all right! That's why I'm calling."

"If you're after the first million-dollar gift, you called the wrong number, Pastor." *[They chuckle again.]*

"No, that's not why I'm calling. But just like the preaching deal, I'll keep that in mind too. *[They laugh.]*

"I've kept that conversation in the back of my mind all this time. You see, I'm convinced that our new program really needs a guide with vision, interest, and conviction for the endowment program. It's going to be important to our ministries in the future, just as it will be to growing faithful disciples in our church right now. You have that vision, interest, and conviction, and it'll be key to the success of our program. So I'm really calling to ask you to pray about serving as the first chair of the committee."

"Well, speaking of chairs, I may need to sit down in one for a minute. You know, I've been on a lot of committees in our church over the years—gosh, it seems like just about all of them—but I've never wanted to be the guy up front. I get sort of anxious when I have to talk to a group."

"But I know, John, that you have a passion for getting this program started. That's what we really need. You're one of the most trusted members of our church. You said that you're not comfortable talking to a group, but I've seen you in a lot of meetings when you're able to help other people see different perspectives and bring understanding when the group has been sort of lost. John, when you speak, people listen. That's what we need in the leader of the new endowment committee."

"Well, I guess you're right about how I like to do things with groups—sort of listen awhile and then try to clarify what I'm hearing."

"And John, because you've been here for so long, you know a lot of the older members of the congregation and can really communicate with them as well. I tell you, you're the man we need to lead this endowment committee."

"You know, Pastor, I love our church, and you know I'll do just about anything to help it. So I'll tell you what. I'll be willing to do what you asked me to do, and that is to pray about being chair of the new committee. I'm not comfortable right now with the idea, but I'm willing to pray."

"I can tell you, John, that the committee on lay leadership prayed before we started talking about asking anyone to participate in this group. We were unanimous that I should call you just as soon as I could and ask that you pray about leading our church family this way. And I'm glad that you're willing to pray about it as well."

"I've prayed myself through a lot of situations in my life, so I know prayer works."

"While you're praying, John, would you also pray for Bill, Carolyn, and Mickey? They're the others whom the lay committee wants to ask to serve on the endowment committee. And, of course, we'll want to keep Gloria, Ralph, and Hazel involved after all the knowledge and awareness that they have accumulated while serving on the task group. If I were a betting man, I'd be willing to bet right now that every one of them will say 'yes' when they know that you'll be leading the group."

"Well, you're nice to say that. And I'll pray for them as well. And I want to pray for Donna too, because at the board meeting the other evening, I was thinking she'd be a fine member of the new committee. Because of her work, she knows something about planned giving, and that knowledge could really help us."

"You know, John, I think you're just as right as you can be. She'd be a great addition to the committee. We know we're going to have plenty of work to go around, and Donna's familiarity with planned giving would be a tremendous help."

"I guess I'd better get to praying. You've given God quite a challenge to talk me into doing this. But I'll tell you next Sunday morning what I think I need to do."

"That's perfect, my friend. Would you like to have a prayer as we finish up?"

"I would, Pastor, and I appreciate your asking."

"Almighty God, John and I want to thank you tonight for our friendship and kinship in Christ. We want to thank you for the challenges that you give us and for the guidance that we can trust as we make important decisions in our lives. Bless our whole church family as we take on this new adventure and begin to prepare for the generations that are yet to become a part of our church family. And thank you, God, for John—for his good spirit and willing heart. Speak to him in these days ahead, and guide him as your beloved disciple as he seeks to discern your will for him. This we pray, God, in the name of our Lord and Savior, Jesus Christ. Amen."

"Thank you, Pastor. You lead us well. Good night."

"Good night, my friend."

• • •

Even though this is a fictitious conversation, it highlights several critical elements of developing an effective team to lead the creative giving emphasis in the congregation. Foremost is the key engagement of the pastor. An endowment program is virtually doomed to oblivion without the pastor's willingness to be a key player in planning and implementing the program. This is not a point at which the pastor can simply agree passively to the effort or consider it the laity's project. The pastor must be willing to invest time, energy, and wise counsel in shaping, implementing, and promoting the program.

The pastor is the key teacher of Christian stewardship in the congregation. With the pastor's guidance, the committee becomes the leaven in the congregation. This biblical and theological foundation affects the entire church's understanding of the importance of creative giving to assure quality, effectiveness, and relevance of the congregation's ministries in future decades. To a large extent, it is the pastor's role to interpret the breadth of Christian stewardship, and that includes managing assets accumulated in estates from every household in the congregation.

In *Faith and Money*,[1] we recommended that the pastor cultivate creative planned giving by making at least one visit every month to households with the highest potential to give during their lifetimes and/or through their estates. This can best be charted out for a multi-year period, so that growth and follow-up can be maintained. Confidential "conversation notes" that the pastor "religiously" writes after each visit can provide the context for future conversations and assure continuity when there is a pastoral change.

The pastor's intentional remembering of things church members say about planned giving, along with these written notes, can serve to initiate or strengthen the program tremendously. In the conversation above, the pastor remembered the interest that John had shown in getting an endowment program underway. There is no substitute for a pastor's good memory about people and conversations, which can only be enhanced by systematic note-keeping.

A second key component of the conversation between John and the pastor is the essential role of at least one respected layperson in the congregation who grasps the necessity and urgency of a creative giving program. An effective program is not pastorally driven; it is lay-driven, with high pastoral participation.

The conversation also points out the need for a committee that represents the diversity of the congregation and includes some of its most respected members. Committee members must have track records of being among the most generous contributors to the church. Their generosity will demonstrate that stewardship is a personal and/or familial priority in their lives and values. It is not simply a mindset meant to apply to others or that might be adopted "when they can afford it."

Further, the committee members need to be potential respondents who will be able to declare, "We have included the church in our estate plan," or "We have established a charitable gift annuity that will eventually benefit the church," or "We have established an endowment that will perpetuate our vision and commitment to always having a strong ministry to children, both in our church and in the neighborhood," or "It was truly a blessing when John and I filled out the Declaration of Intent the other evening."

The conversation between John and his pastor also shows that there must be a congenial relationship between the pastor and the members of the committee, as well as a strong tie and an affirmative relationship between the committee and the church's governing board. The governing board must usually be trained in and informed on creative giving, and, typically, members of the governing body are prime candidates for planned gifts, because they love their church and often have longstanding relationships with the congregation.

Part of the role of the creative giving committee is to keep the governing body well informed, to be responsive to questions that emerge, and to educate new members of the body about the nature and importance of creative giving to both the present and the future of the church.

Seldom does congregational leadership oppose a creative giving program. The leaders first need to catch the vision of the program's potential in order to grow stronger stewards in the current congregation and to develop financial stability for future congregations. It's easy for a governing board to understand that the current financial capacity might be much stronger if a creative giving program had been established ten or twenty years ago.

Another matter disclosed in the conversation was the engagement of allied professionals who plan and guide the creative giving program. This might include attorneys familiar with tax matters and estate planning, certified public accountants, persons acquainted with the ins and outs of life insurance, certified financial planners, bank trust officers, planned giving professionals in other organizations, and those familiar with approaches to effective marketing.

Some of these individuals may be internal; they are members of the congregation and are available to serve. Others might be non-members or external advisors to the committee. In any event, the committee must adopt a policy for itself and for any advisors in order to avoid any conflicts of interest. Neither the committee nor its advisors can ever be in a position to expect or receive any gain, financial or otherwise, from participating in the work of the committee—with the exception, perhaps, of great personal satisfaction.

Although it might seem to go without saying, it is imperative that every member of the committee and every advisor be able to maintain confidentiality. Some of the information to which the members might become privy can be deeply personal and private, and the confidentiality of this information must be protected without exception.

A final element evident in the conversation is that the workings of the committee are deeply spiritual. Prayer is at the center of all conversations held and all decisions made. As with any undertaking associated with stewardship, the faithful giving and receiving of God's provisions is a spiritual matter to each individual and family in the congregation. The teachings about creative giving, the materials that might be prepared for distribution, the seminars that might be conducted, the presentations that are made to various church bodies, and the words that are written for newsletters or spoken from the pulpit must always be rooted and grounded in God's love.

Oh yes, and members of the committee must have the spiritual gift of patience. Seldom do new programs realize immediate rewards. The committee's work is to teach, to plant seeds, and to interpret the impact of planned gifts on ministry. It is at this point that the capacity to envision, design, and manage multi-year plans must be employed.

Note

1. Reeves and Tyler, *Faith and Money*.

CHAPTER 15

Approaches for Working with Churches

While we can identify leadership roles generically, the application of leadership varies dramatically. And just as God made each of us with various gifts and graces, communities of faith have their unique cultures and relationships as well.

A couple of years ago, we decided to develop an approach that could be replicated across the state. Our "model church" program was to apply some of what we had learned from past experiences asking churches to develop planned giving programs in their communities. The three initial pastors were vaguely familiar with the concept and stated a desire to start the effort. The churches served towns of 18,000, 72,000, and 110,000. The size of the congregations reflected the towns they served. The two smaller churches had previously been exposed to the idea of planned giving and had received planned gifts.

Two of the pastors asked members of the financial services industry to lead their efforts, while the third asked a financially savvy businessman. The smaller churches selected males in their thirties and forties, while the largest chose a female nearing retirement. All three individuals were articulate, respected, and dedicated members of their respective churches.

There was a one-on-one meeting first with the individual chairs. A second meeting briefed each of the committees on the need to address the issue and on the potential in their respective churches. The same collateral material was used, and the same plan and calendar were suggested.

All of the committees reacted positively and indicated they would be going forward.

Six months later, the largest church received three planned gifts as a result of a luncheon presentation. The middle-sized church held a seminar that no one attended, including the committee chair. The smallest church had not yet been able to reconvene its committee.

Why the difference? All of pastors expressed support of the effort, the chairs were equally knowledgeable, and the congregations were strong and generous. The results, however, were drastically different.

The Pastor

The pastor is the gatekeeper. Very little in any faith community is successful without the pastor's true support. If it involves money, the pastor must be fully engaged and not simply pay lip service to the effort.

This does not mean that pastors should chair the committees—they should not. Pastors, however, must believe in their committees enough to support their leadership choices, attend events, and donate their own money. After all, how much does it affect our lifestyles to add a codicil to a will leaving a planned gift after we are no longer here to spend the money? Yet how much more effective it is when we say to someone, "Try it. I did."

The Chair

If the pastor is the gatekeeper, then the chair is the force that pushes the project through after the gate has been opened. The pastor is the spiritual leader whose support is critical; however, the pastor cannot personally lead every effort. He or she needs a champion—an advocate who is willing to take some of the burden of leadership and be dedicated to seeing something through to success.

Don't make the mistake of selecting individuals with the most titles, professional designations, or expensive toys. Not only are they on everyone's hit list, but these things don't accurately describe someone's heart for the church. They will have demonstrated their hearts by being active in other areas of ministry. They must be respected by the membership but not overburdened with prior responsibilities. The need for good communication skills will often bring forth the names of teachers, coaches, and salespeople. And they will be giving financially to the church.

Leadership

For both the pastor and the chair, leadership is a necessary virtue.

In her book, *Jesus CEO*, Laurie Beth Jones compares Jesus' leadership style to that found in the contemporary business world.[1] While many people may neither want to emulate current business magnates nor be able to act exactly as Christ, Jones describes some encouraging leadership principles. In two of the three areas describing the strengths of Jesus' leadership techniques, several points can be directly applied by church leaders developing a planned giving program.

Strength of Action

Jesus took action. The pastor is the gatekeeper of virtually everything that moves forward in a church. Take action.

Jesus had a plan. Use the five-year plan provided in Don Joiner's *Creating a Climate for Giving* or one of the many others available.[2]

Jesus formed a team. Establish a group of church members with the express purpose of developing an endowment in your church.

Jesus was visible. There was no doubt about where Jesus stood. Stewardship is a spiritual matter, and the pastor and endowment chair are the spiritual leaders of the church. Be visible in your support.

Jesus took the long view. Americans live in a world of instant gratification. Planned giving development is the final area of stewardship that most churches have not dealt with well, if at all. As with so many things a church does, this effort begins with planting seeds. It takes time for the seeds to grow, but the harvest can be greatly rewarding.

Strength of Relationships

Jesus gave people a vision of something larger than themselves. Endowment donors often use accumulated assets to make much larger gifts than had been possible from just their income streams. They want to make a bigger difference with their lives. Show them a vision.

Jesus educated people. People must learn that they are able to make planned gifts. Sermons, newsletter articles, bulletin inserts, testimonials, and seminars all provide education. Teach them.

Jesus set an example for people. Leaders lead by example. Make a planned gift.

Jesus prayed for people. All church efforts need this support. After all, this is about the future of the church ministry.

Jesus kept urging the people on. As with any long-term project, a leader acts as a mentor to those who are responsible for the details.

Committee Members

Committee members will look very similar to the people you consider for the chair position. They too must have demonstrated hearts for the church.

Have you noticed that the more you are involved with something, the greater love you have for it? For most of us, the greater our love for something, the more willing we are to give of ourselves. People acknowledge their belief in the value of ministries by doing the things that a denomination asks of all new members: to support it with their time, their talents, and their treasures.

Prospective committee members will already be involved in the church ministries. The church has already seen them use their worldly experiences and expertise to improve existing programs.

And they will already be giving to the church financially *in a significant way.* A significant way is not a certain number of dollars; it is a substantial part of their incomes. If they are not giving significantly of their incomes, why would anyone think they would give of their assets?

These people lend their credibility to the program. They do not have to become experts in wills and bequests, charitable gift annuities, charitable remainder trusts, or life estates. They do not have to be wealthy or beg people for money.

They will become familiar with the advantages offered by planned giving. They will understand that everyone can make a difference, regardless of wealth. They will place their reputations and relationships on the line in order to open doors to a flow of information.

Planned giving deals with a very sensitive matter to most Americans. It deals with their money and how to use it effectively for others. Teaching this spiritual concept is art, not science.

Notes

1. Laurie Beth Jones, *Jesus CEO: Using Ancient Wisdom for Visionary Leadership* (New York: Hyperion, 1995).

2. Joiner, 92–94.

CHAPTER 16

Approaches for Working with Individuals

In his book, *Wit, Wisdom & Moxie*, Jerold Panas tells us the U.S. is home to one hundred thousand men and women who are one hundred years of age or older. He goes on to state, "One thing of particular interest. Those who provide for charity in their estate plans live longer than the general public—six years beyond the Actuarial Tables."[1]

No, this is not a suggestion to promise donors longer lives in return for gifts. But it does tell us about donors. They care about something beyond themselves. It is an analogous reminder to address the individual's need to give in appreciation for things received or to leave a legacy, not our ministries' need to survive. Remember the lady described in Chapter 9 who said, "You don't know how good this makes me feel!"

Identification

Creative giving donors are people who have hearts for the ministries in which they are active. They may not be the most outspoken, but their actions reflect their interests. They are active supporters with their time, talents, and money. If they have seen the benefits of their ministries today, they are more likely to see how their ministries can benefit others in the future.

While we want to offer everyone involved in the church the opportunity to make a planned gift, not everyone will be interested or able. Part of the planned giving committee's responsibility is to ascertain which individuals are most likely to be open to and benefit from making planned gifts.

Who in your organization fits the following descriptions?

- Members of the endowment committee
- Current staff members, both professional and volunteer
- Members holding key leadership positions
- Current and former members of the governing body (board)
- Active leaders/volunteers of specialized areas of service
- Active leaders in Sunday school
- Active long-term members of the church
- Active members of the women's group
- Active members of the men's group
- Members who serve in capacities beyond the local church
- Members who have already made planned gifts
- Current and former long-term staff members, now retired
- Members who have been especially affected by particular services
- Members with histories of loyal giving
- Members who have made sacrificial gifts to capital campaigns
- Members who have made frequent memorial gifts
- Members age sixty and above
- Single members
- Members who are married with no children
- Families of those whom the church has recognized through naming opportunities (*i.e.*, chapel, bells, classrooms)

The legacy of Walt Disney is one of bringing joy to multiple generations through his vision and imagination. The Disney name badge encourages visitors to "Imagine the Possibilities." Wouldn't this be a fitting challenge to those you have identified as potential donors?

Donors want to learn if it is possible for them to make planned gifts even if they are not wealthy. Can they do it and still provide for their families? Is it expensive and complicated? Most of all, they want it to address their hearts' desires. They need you to educate them on the possibilities. And they need you to ask for gifts.

Developing Relationships

Have you ever had a best friend or fallen in love? Do you remember how that relationship developed? You discovered shared interests or talents by asking questions. You knew they liked you because they listened to your replies.

The same is true when working with donors. Ethically, it is imperative to learn the donor's interests and intent. Personally, it is often the beginning of an interesting and rewarding friendship.

How do you get to know anyone? You ask about them. You listen for personal details, particularly those with which you resonate. Have they always lived where they do now? Where did they grow up? What do they do for a living? Where did they go to school? Do they have any children or grandchildren? What do they do with their spare time? How did they come to be connected with your ministry? What excites them most about what is going on now? What would they like to see happen in the future?

Donors will be people who have already expressed support for the programs and ministries you represent. They will have already given of their time and money.

Financial Concerns

Since planned giving involves a gift of assets, donors will probably express some common concerns. Perhaps they would like to make a difference but are unsure of how to do it or even if they can afford to do something. All of us with any charitable intent struggle with balancing the needs of our families against the needs of the ministries that warm our hearts.

What financial details would assist in making a good decision? What about income? What is the amount and source of potential donors' incomes? Are they still acquiring assets, or liquidating them in order to meet living expenses? What are these assets? Do they own any investment real estate, stocks, or bonds? Do they have life insurance, disability insurance, and/or long-term care insurance? How about retirement plans?

The answers to these questions provide hints as to how much they may be able to give, as well as the best methods or vehicles to recommend. Most people just think of writing a check, which immediately reduces their usable income. Do they know that some gifts may generate increased streams of income? Some gifts don't ever affect income because they do not take effect until after their lifetimes. If they have lived lives of generosity—perhaps giving certain percentages of their incomes to various causes—would they like to do the same with their accumulated assets? Do they realize what they can accomplish with beneficiary clauses to life insurance policies or retirement plans?

Which family members and professional advisors should be involved in the decision? Do you have the authority to visit with them directly?

Approached in a caring, sensitive manner, this conversation should serve to expand and strengthen your relationships with donors. After all, if we were mere acquaintances, we would not be so interested in their lives and dreams, and they would not share this much personal detail. It is virtually impossible to share this type of decision with someone without first developing a relationship that both sides value.

Communication

The hope is that these discussions will lead to a decision that benefits both the donor and your ministry. Be certain that donors and anyone involved in the decision understand the gift. It is a gift. Once an irrevocable gift is given, the asset is no longer under the donor's control.

If it is a type of life income gift, emphasize to whom the income goes, when it stops, and whether there is a secondary income beneficiary. Do they understand it to pay a fixed dollar amount, or will the amount vary depending on the value of the trust corpus?

One confused donor was surprised but silently enjoyed the increasing number of dollars he received from his trust for several years. The first year the amount declined, however, he called to ask why. He explained, "As long as it was more than I expected, I saw no reason to call."

Is the income taxable, or is part of it tax-free? A charitable gift has a motive too pure to be sullied by miscommunication. Err on the side of too much information.

Follow Up

Once the transaction has been completed, recognize the donor, and stay in touch. Keep donors apprised of the progress of the "possibilities" they have decided to support. If it is a scholarship, let them know who the student recipients are. If it is a lecture series, invite them to the lectures. Tell them of the progress the program has made or the number of people served. Let them know how they made a difference.

Donors make great referrals. Most of us like to talk about our successes. If we get a good buy or make a good decision, don't we like to tell others? Donors will too.

Further, people generally hang around others with similar interests. Studies show that approximately 85 percent of those who have made a planned gift will make another one—either to your institution or another.

When the retired schoolteacher's husband died, she became even more involved in her charitable interests. I noticed her comfortable but modest home on my visits. Her first charitable gift annuity was followed by a second, third, fourth, and fifth. When I commented on the increasingly shorter intervals of time between gifts, she explained that she did not yet need the additional income, so she just "saved it up" for the next gift.

Do what friends do. Stay in touch with an occasional note, birthday card, or telephone call. Invite them to whatever gathering, luncheon, or open house you think might be of any interest. Send them copies of articles they might enjoy. Isn't it great when friends do that for you?

Whether it is the first gift or the seventeenth, we must let our donors know that we need and appreciate their planned gifts. Remember that people give to people. It is not the brochure, website, or seminar they give to, but the person representing the ministry that has touched their hearts.

Notes

1. From *Wit, Wisdom & Moxie: A Fundraiser's Compendium of Wrinkles, Strategies, and Admonitions That Really Work*, by Jerold Panas, page 154. © 2002 Bonus Books.

CHAPTER 17

Marketing Planned Giving

It is suggested that adults in America are bombarded with fifteen hundred to three thousand commercial messages per day, counting newspapers, magazines, radio, television, and the Internet.[1] Children are subjected to even more. How do we get through the blitz?

As an established charity, you start off with a great advantage. People already know who you are, and they appreciate your work, as evidenced by volunteering their time and/or their financial support. You know who they are. Communities of faith have audiences on a weekly basis.

Whatever the cause, the people supporting your work share a common interest. It may be research, education, conservation, or spirituality. Your marketing message must speak to that shared value. Don't make the mistake of focusing on tax benefits. This is not a tax shelter—this has heart!

Estate taxes? Social capital? Ninety-eight percent of Americans do not have estates large enough for them to worry about estate taxes.[2] With the ever-changing predictions regarding the demise of the estate tax, no one really knows. If you are focusing on the heart value—the intent of the donor—it generally doesn't really matter what happens in 2010.

Who Is Our Audience?

Do the people you work with understand planned giving and the role it can play? While often overlooked, the very people who talk with the members of your church on a daily basis, answer the telephone, or greet them at the front door may not understand planned giving. Making a presentation to your staff not only raises their awareness, but it gives you good practice as well.

How about your governing board? Its members were recognized as leaders and supporters of the cause when asked to serve. Do they understand planned giving? Have they made planned gifts? It is certainly easy to do, isn't it?

Schedule a regular time during board meetings to relate a donor story, and use it to explain a form of gift. You are combining instruction and motivation.

Work your way through the board. Take each member to lunch to develop relationships. As you educate them on the value of planned giving, ask who they think might benefit from making a gift. Will they be willing to introduce you to that person? Take them to a thank-you lunch with a donor who has made a planned gift. All of this can pave the way to eventually talking to them about planned gifts of their own.

Who are the people you serve? For a hospital, it might be patients or the families of those it has helped. A university has graduates; a research center has people who have benefited from new treatments or medicines. A community of faith has members of its congregation.

Professional advisors go by many names. They may be called accountants, attorneys, insurance agents, stockbrokers, trust officers, or financial planners. Get to know these people in your community. You may need to call on them for their professional services. They would probably love to speak at your educational seminars. They may be surprised to learn you are helping some of their clients make planned gifts to your cause.

Like anyone, professionals respond to someone who provides something of value. Almost all of them have continuing educational requirements. Can you hold a workshop that qualifies for those credits? Do you receive a truly useful e-mail newsletter that you can forward to them on a weekly or monthly basis? Do they know about your website? Does it offer easy-to-understand information on the various giving vehicles or gift calculators?

A word needs to be said here about professional ethics. True professionals are governed by codes of ethics. The same is true for you. The first Standard of Practice in "Model Standards of Practice for the Charitable Gift Planner" states, "The principal basis for making a charitable gift should be a desire on the part of the donor to support the work of charitable institutions."[3] Remember, it is a heart decision.

How Do We Reach People?

In their book, *Holy $moke! Whatever Happened to Tithing?*, J. Clif Christopher and Herb Mather emphasize the need for "education, more education, and continuous education."[4] They go on to say, "Successful churches that receive a number of planned gifts offer frequent teaching seminars and mailings regarding the variety of possibilities members should consider as good stewards of their resources."[5]

Seminars

Make the first seminar a broad-based educational one. A common practice is to spend the first year focusing on bequests. But remember, we are not the first ones to talk about planned giving. Universities, hospitals, and others have been mailing information on various gift vehicles to our people for years. Why delay another year to encourage these types of gifts, particularly if our people are already giving them? They need to know you want the gift. Ask!

I had just finished a luncheon presentation on the benefits of planned giving when an energetic lady standing about four feet eight inches tall approached me. "Why, honey, I have been giving these gift annuity things to that children's home up north for years. I didn't know my church would be interested in them." I quickly reached over to steady my visibly shaken host, the local pastor.

Although someone may approach you immediately, as the diminutive lady did, it will usually take time. You are introducing yourself, establishing trust, and beginning the educational effort. You are sowing the seeds for future gifts. Experience has shown that food enhances the appeal an informational seminar. The purpose is to inform your audience such possibilities exist, let them know you can help, and ask for the gift.

After the seminar, write each person a note thanking him or her for attending and offering free consultation or examples. Several vendors offer software that uses the donor's individual information to produce attractive illustrations that explain the various gift vehicles. Offer to add potential donors to your mailing list for "no cost, no obligation" planned giving information. It is important to build trust with prospective donors.

If the seminar does produce a request for consultation, waste no time. Arrange a meeting the following day or as soon as possible. It took courage to make the request, so don't treat it casually and let donors think they may have been wrong to ask. Remember the Golden Rule: treat others as you would like to be treated.

Collateral Material

Perhaps the first piece of material to acquire is one that explains planned giving in a brief, understandable fashion. Sometimes called a "leave behind," the one we use gives the major points and benefits of bequests, charitable gift annuities, charitable remainder trusts, and life estates. Use your logo to personalize your material. It can be mailed, handed out at seminars, and used at personal visits.

Relatively inexpensive direct-mail pieces highlighting the advantages of the different types of planned giving vehicles are available from various vendors. Consider a regular mailing, perhaps quarterly, rotating the topics.

Fixed income from charitable gift annuities appeals to some, while others prefer the potential of asset growth through trusts. The need for controlling their assets leads some people to bequests, while the opportunity to involve their children in philanthropy leads others to donor-advised funds.

Never waste postage. This doesn't mean don't mail; it means always include an insert describing a planned gift vehicle in anything you send out. Do you send out receipts for annual gifts? Enclose a piece describing the benefits of charitable gift annuities. Mail a regular newsletter about your program. Insert an invitation to join your planned giving society. Donor stories can be used with great success. One good source for ideas is *Planned Giving Today*'s "Marketing Reprintable," which can be found on the inside back page of each issue.

Always include a response card. Make it easy to use and mail. In addition to places for name, address, telephone number, and e-mail, offer some choices. Examples include:

I have already included _____ in my estate plans.
Please send me the booklet _____.
I am interested in obtaining an income stream for life.
Please send me future issues of the *Planned Giving* newsletter.

How do you open your mail? I stand over the trashcan as I thumb through ours, so I can drop envelopes in without even opening them. But what about a postcard? Even if I drop it directly into the trash, it still communicates a least a portion of its message to me.

We tried postcards recently after being frustrated by the low response rates to other direct-mail efforts. The results were amazing! Responses to the same mailing list went from two or three to over fifty. And they were cheaper and easier to produce and mail.

Keep Reminders in Front of Them

Factoids are one- to three-sentence facts your people will find interesting and amusing. They relate to your mission and quantify how you are addressing the need in which both your supporters and institution are interested. Drop them in anywhere—in letters, ads, statements, thank-you notes, and invitations.

One-liners are provocative one-sentence questions that can easily fit into any publication you send out. You have probably seen "Have you remembered us in your will?" more times than you recall. How about:

- Every woman needs a will. Does your wife have one?
- Make a big difference with little installments. (life insurance)
- Inherited IRAs are taxed unless you leave them to us.
- Income for you now helps us later. (life income gift)

The answer to the question of timing is "yes." At this very moment, we are all in some cycle of our lives—birth, school, graduation, marriage, new job, retirement, or death. Seldom, however, are our life cycles in sync with each other. The only answer is to be persistent. Keep reminders in front of people throughout the year.

Websites

The 2003 *Planned Giving Today* readership survey indicated that 80 percent of its subscribers had planned giving websites. Forty-five percent could cite specific gifts that resulted from their sites.[6]

Several vendors offer turnkey websites that supply most of the information you need. Compare several to decide which one fits your constituency best. But to be successful, the site itself must be marketed. Consider a brochure describing how to find and navigate your site.

Time Out

You have to see people to get to know them. Remember, people give to people, and they don't give to people they don't know. This is the fun part, but you will have to be intentional about it. Just as any relationship takes time to grow, this one will too.

How many times have you decided to spend a substantial amount of money the first time you thought about it? Schedule regular visits to see the people whom you think are the most interested in planned gifts. Remember, since everyone will not become a donor, numbers do matter.

Say "Thank You"

Recognition societies are an easy way to thank donors. Do you have one for planned giving donors? Qualifications can include remembering your organization in their wills, adding you as a beneficiary to life insurance policies, retirement plans, or as the ultimate beneficiary of charitable gift annuities or trusts. Some charities require copies of documents or minimum dollar amounts to qualify for some form of recognition, but that is not the standard.

Put It All Together

Make a plan—a multi-year plan. You can't do everything at once, but you can do anything over time. Budget constraints and job responsibilities make planning a necessity.

Stay Fresh

Take advantage of any opportunity to broaden your knowledge. The National Committee on Planned Giving has chapters throughout the country. They hold a national conference each year with lectures and seminars that are full of ideas and inspiration. Many vendors offer educational seminars. Watch what your university, community foundation, or any of the national charities do. Remember, imitation is the sincerest form of flattery.

Notes

1. Sine, *Mustard Seed*, 89.

2. United for a Fair Economy, "Who Pays the Estate Tax?" http://www.faireconomy.org/estatetax/ETWhoPays.html (accessed April 22, 2005).

3. From "Model Standards of Practice for the Charitable Gift Planner," by the National Committee on Planned Giving and the American Council on Gift Annuities, May 7, 1991. Revised 1999. Copyright © 2005 National Committee on Planned Giving. http://www.ncpg.org/ethics_standards/model_stds.asp?section=7

4. From *Holy $moke! Whatever Happened to Tithing?*, by J. Clif Christopher and Herb Mather, page 78. © 1999 Discipleship Resources.

5. *Ibid.*

6. *Planned Giving Today*, "2003 Readership Survey," Edmonds, Washington.

TIMELINE FOR PLANNING AND CONDUCTING YOUR ESTATE AND GIFT PLANNING SEMINAR

A. Four Months Prior to Scheduled Seminar

1. Finalize plans with the person(s) selected to lead the seminar. These professionals might include one or more persons from the judicatory foundation, a local tax attorney who can address issues about estate planning matters and various gift options, a certified public accountant who can present information about tax issues, and other professionals whose leadership is considered relevant and important.

2. Identify and enlist the persons to initially serve on the planning committee, and engage them in the projects that follow.

3. Develop a list of the names, addresses, and telephone numbers of all members and active non-members sixty years of age and older, plus all members and active non-members forty to sixty years of age who have no children.

4. Determine who will prepare the letter of invitation. Each letter should have an inside address and a personalized salutation. Each letter will be signed by two people: the chair of the creative giving committee and one other key official who believes in the urgency of a permanent endowment and in the need for Christian disciples to be responsible stewards of the gifts God provides. Begin drafting the letter for review.

5. Begin drafting a pastor's letter to be sent to all invitees. (The same characteristics for personalization apply to this letter.)

6. Confirm the date, place, meal (or refreshments or heavy hors d'oeuvres), and other arrangements for the seminar. Enlist one person as a site arrangement coordinator who can engage additional persons to assist.

B. **Three Months Prior to Scheduled Seminar**

1. Perfect the list of invitees. Eliminate those who no longer live in area and others for whom an invitation would be inappropriate, *e.g.*, no longer mentally able to make decisions.

2. First drafts of letters are prepared and distributed to the planning committee for review.

3. Choose one to four persons to write four promotional newsletter articles to precede and promote the seminar. Begin preparing articles.

4. Determine whether a member or friend of the congregation has skills as a graphic artist to develop a professional-quality logo to be used on all publications or announcements of the seminar.

5. Balance the planning committee to include a liaison with other congregational bodies, such as the trustees, finance committee, and governing body, if not already represented. Add other members to the planning committee if needed. These are all to be active members of the committee for the purpose of planning and conducting the seminar, and they need to be committed to the ministry potential of the creative giving program. There is typically more to be done than the existing committee can reliably undertake. Besides, adding more personnel is an effective way of enhancing ownership in the seminar.

C. **Week 8 Before the Scheduled Seminar**

Week 8 Begins: _____, _____

1. Prepare 5" x 8" index cards with name, address, and telephone number of each invitee/couple. Include spouses by name, even if not members of the congregation. Mailing labels can be used.

2. Authors of newsletter articles confer to determine approach, emphasis, and style of articles.

3. Inform any existing congregational prayer groups of the plans for the seminar, and request that they regularly include the planning committee, congregation, and prospective participants in their prayers.

D. Week 6 Begins: _____, _____

1. Assign every invitee to a member of the planning committee for personal invitation and follow-up. Recognize and honor existing relationships; consider who is the best contact for each invitee. Distribute 5" x 8" index cards to committee members (from C.1. above). Maintain a master list of all planning committee members and the invitees they are to contact.

2. Prepare all letters for mailing with individual signatures, hand-addressed envelopes, and first class stamps.

3. Determine whether any invitations should be hand-delivered, and if so, who should deliver them. (*Hand-delivered* means making an appointment and taking the letter by the home or office, *not* passing it out on Sunday morning or at another congregational gathering.)

4. All four newsletter articles are drafted, reviewed, and finalized.

E. Week 5 Begins: _____, _____

Newsletter articles submitted for publication with clear indication of order, dates of publication, who to contact if there are questions, etc.

F. Week 4 Begins: _____, _____

1. Mail or hand-deliver letter #1 from the planning committee.

2. Publish newsletter article #1.

G. **Week 3 Begins:** _____, _____

1. Mail or hand-deliver pastor's letter.

2. Confer with presenter to determine space, audio visual, and display requirements.

3. Reconfirm all plans for place, special arrangements, audio visual equipment, food, etc.

4. Re-contact existing prayer groups, requesting that they hold the planning committee, congregation, and prospective participants in their prayers.

5. Publish newsletter article #2. Include invitation to call church office if letter of invitation was not received and invitee wishes to attend. Church office will need to prepare letter, get signatures, and mail, or forward information to a member of the planning committee, who will oversee this task immediately.

6. Layperson announces the seminar during worship service(s).

H. **Week 2 Begins:** _____, _____

1. Planning committee calls every invitee to encourage attendance, answer questions, and determine approximate participation. Make notes on cards for later reference. Report any pastoral concerns to pastor immediately.

2. Publish newsletter article #3. (Include invitation to call church office if letter of invitation was not received and invitee wishes to attend. See note G.5.)

3. Pastor announces the seminar during worship service(s).

I. **Week 1 Begins:** _____, _____

1. Callers report attendance projections to site coordinator for arrangements, seating, food, etc.

2. Late in the week, callers telephone to remind each invitee who has indicated definite or possible plans for attendance.

3. Prepare nametags for all possible attendees, and have extras for unexpected attendees.

4. Publish newsletter article #4.

5. Layperson announces the seminar during worship service(s).

J. **Week 0: Day of Event or Just Before the Event On:** _____ ,
    _____

1. Finalize space setting and arrangements. Include reception table with prepared nametags.

2. Chair of creative giving committee or planning committee announces the seminar during worship service(s).

3. All committee members report to room twenty minutes early to serve as hosts and hostesses.

4. Late in the week, planning committee contacts all attendees to acknowledge them, answer or refer questions, or encourage follow-up, as appropriate.

K. **Week +1 Begins:** _____ , _____

1. Planning committee meets to debrief from seminar. Determine next steps to follow up with both attendees and those unable to attend. Forward meeting notes with ideas, suggestions, and information to presenter.

2. Collect all contact cards with notes for later reference. Determine where they will be kept. Note the information in meeting minutes.

3. Pastor and chairs of creative giving committee and planning committee review all note cards to assure that each person is "complete" with the process. Plan any additional steps/contacts that would assist each person to have all information, etc., that might be desired.

"HOW DO YOU GET PEOPLE THERE?"

A friend of mine asked me to come to his church to talk about creative giving. He and his wife had established a life income gift that they were enjoying. "I grew up in this church," he told me. "I know these people, and I know that some of them would benefit from hearing about it. How many people do you need to have attend for it to be worth your while?"

Although there is no minimum required number, he knew a trip to his church involved a five-hour drive for me. When he asked if thirty people would be a large enough audience, I assured him that it would.

Thirty-two people attended the luncheon. Afterwards, I asked him how he had gotten such a good crowd. "Weren't nothing," he said. "I just personally invited each one."

This is the secret. In today's busy world, think of all the notices and invitations we receive. Many of us hide behind our voice mail to screen the calls from telemarketers and survey takers; however, when someone you respect asks you to do something, don't you give it serious consideration?

Chances are, potential donors will too. If you believe in the effort—and you should if you accepted the responsibility—be bold, and personally contact people to say:

"I need a favor.

"The pastor asked me to join a couple of other people to look into something he/she called creative giving. It has to do with money and the church, something like financial planning, but from a spiritual perspective.

"I have learned there are some things that we average people can do that will pay us attractive rates of income or help us save on capital gains or income taxes. We can actually help ourselves, our families, and our church.

"We are getting together to discuss some of these ideas over (lunch/dinner, etc.) on (date) at the church. I think it will be interesting and worthwhile. No products will be sold, and there will be no request for money. You can leave your checkbook at home. You won't be asked to divulge private information, either. I have learned some things, and I think you could too.

"The favor I need to ask is—will you come?"

CHAPTER 18

Models and Stories

for some congregations, the process of learning comes through what might be referred to as the "school of hard knocks." Usually this occurs because of inadequate planning. This is particularly true of small congregations that do not foresee the need for a creative giving program. To their way of thinking, such a program is for larger, wealthier congregations situated in urban and suburban areas.

The myth that needs to be debunked is that a creative giving program is for congregations that are somehow "better off than ours." It's a rare congregation that does not need a creative giving program, even though, in smaller congregations, it need not be as extensive as it is in larger congregations. Perhaps this will become clearer by telling some stories and painting some personal, family, and congregational portraits.

A congregation in a small farming community received word that a former resident and church member had included the church in her will. Her declining health had required her to relocate from the community several decades earlier in order to be closer to family.

Until the move, she had lived most of her life in the community and had been a faithful member of the church. Because of her long absence, though, many of the younger members of the church did not know her. No one expected that her estate or the bequest to the church would be large. To their amazement, the bequest was almost a quarter of a million dollars!

Because the church did not have a framework in place for receiving, managing, and benefiting from these new funds, the money soon became a stumbling block for the congregation. There were many ideas about how the funds should be used. Due to the differences of opinion, relationships began to suffer.

Eventually, the church decided to use a portion of the funds for renovating several parts of the church building. The major portion of the funds was invested with the church's judicatory foundation. But still the disagreements persisted in this small church family.

Some saw no need to protect the asset for the long term because the congregation would probably go out of existence in another decade anyway. Others saw the gift as a substitute for the personal and familial giving by members of the congregation. Some wanted distributions from the invested funds to provide for ministries that the congregation could not otherwise afford. Others believed that the distributions should be large enough to cover all of the denominational apportionments and requests, and current members could cover the cost of local operations and salaries. Still others wanted the fund to provide for the upkeep of the sturdy but aging buildings.

It took several years, many long and heated discussions, and three treasurers—each of whom resigned from weariness over the church members' wrangling—for resolutions to emerge and some degree of harmony to be restored. These resolutions now provide for regular distributions that both support the ministries of the congregation and protect the remaining corpus of the fund for the longevity of the church.

One of the lessons this congregation learned was that while money does not always bring out the best in people, a large bequest may bring out some of the inactive members to express their opinions and vote at meetings. The moral of the story is that no congregation is too small to have basic policies in place that allow for receiving, managing, and using bequests, even if the congregation chooses not to have a full-fledged creative giving program.

The chair of an endowment committee in a medium-sized congregation in an urban area called to schedule an estate and planned giving seminar at his church. The congregation already had several permanent funds invested with the judicatory foundation, and the chair and his wife had established a charitable gift annuity several years previously. The congregation, though, had never had a seminar such as this, and the chair wanted direction about how to plan an event that would compel couples and individuals to attend.

A four-month plan of preparation and follow-up was developed with the congregation, and it effectively served to engage the endowment committee, to reach a sizeable number of congregation members in a personal way, and to reduce the potential for misunderstanding the nature of the gathering. It was not just for the rich members of the congregation. It was not just for those who did not have wills. It was not just for those who needed financial counseling. It was not a gathering just to talk about money and death. It was not just to try to coerce folks into giving money to the church. It was not a meeting where people would have to divulge private information about their personal investments and estate plans. These misunderstandings were overcome.

The two-hour session brought together some of the most faithful members and leaders of the congregation for a fruitful time of presentation and discussion. Through these conversations, several individuals and couples learned ways in which they could restructure some of their plans to better serve themselves while they are living and, eventually, to benefit the church that they loved.

The pastor of a medium-sized church in a medium-sized town knew that there were couples and individuals in the congregation who had the potential to make gifts to the church through their estates. While he did not know the extent of their estates, he knew that these people were loyal contributors to the church. It was his estimate, though, that in all likelihood, they had not included the church in their estate plans.

The pastor knew very little about planned giving and nothing about the various instruments that might be available to assist these members. He invited the executive director of the judiciary foundation to come to the community and visit the homes of several of these members across a two-day interval. The visits were friendly, informal, and informative. They were not intended to initially lead to particular gifts from the visited members. They were, however, blessed occasions where loyal church members discovered ways in which the church might serve them through the judiciary foundation.

One gentleman who was visited did, in fact, take the information that was left from that visit, consult with his attorney, and prepare a codicil to his will. When he died a number of months later, he left a gift to the church. This gift allowed for building renovations "sometime in the future" and for the installation of an elevator to be given more immediate attention. His bequest became the stimulus for congregational action and support of a project that had seemed out of reach to them.

Today, there are refurbished classrooms, well-designed and frequently used spaces for youth ministry, and an elevator that allows all church members to reach areas for classes, meetings, and other activities throughout the facility. It was one pastor's vision, along with his awareness that he did not personally have all the information that he needed, that led to the fulfillment of a congregation's long-anticipated dream.

In a county seat in the early 1990s, an older couple was experiencing a growing need to increase their income. They had substantial investments that were producing little in dividends. The particular investments, however, had grown considerably in market value. Selling these assets little by little to increase their income would have meant significant capital gains tax liabilities.

They first read about a charitable gift annuity in the newsletter of the judicatory foundation. In 1994, following conversations with their pastor and with the executive director of the foundation, they gave shares of the stock that were producing little income to the foundation. This gift funded a charitable gift annuity.

The foundation immediately sold the stock for $117,000.00. The couple avoided capital gains taxes on the transaction, and, in fact, received a tax deduction for part of the gift. Because of their ages, the couple received a substantial, dependable income for the remainder of their lives. Part of this was also exempt from income tax.

In early 2002, both of them died only a few weeks apart. From 1994, when the gift annuity was established, to 2002, when they died, the couple had received over $98,000.00 in monthly annuity payments. By way of the written documentation that they had filed with the judicatory foundation, their church received the balance of the fund to establish a new endowment that would support the church ministries beyond the church's budget. This new endowment started with a corpus in excess of $135,000.00!

While foundations operate with different investment programs, and while the returns and growth on investments vary over the years, this couple's experience clearly demonstrates the value of charitable gift annuities, both to the donors and to the church they loved.

Even though they had lived in a number of communities throughout their married lives due to his work in the petroleum industry, another couple decided to retire to an urban area near their daughter. Neither of them had been able to attend college, but both were highly committed to the importance of higher education. They had seen to it that their daughter had the benefit of a college education when she graduated from high school.

During their retirement, the couple became active in First Church. There, the congregation had several endowed scholarships that were presented annually to young members.

Upon the couple's deaths, their daughter became their executor. They had instructed her to tithe the residuum of their estate after all of the bills had been paid and all accounts settled.

Prior to their deaths, the couple's Sunday school class had established a new scholarship fund. While setting up the fund, the class decided that no scholarships would be awarded until the corpus reached a certain level. This was to assure that the amount of each scholarship would be significant enough to make a difference in the recipient's finances. This simple bequest from a loving, generous, and farsighted couple moved the scholarship endowment across the threshold and allowed for the first scholarship to be awarded early the following summer.

Another truly moving part of the story was the joy that the daughter expressed by fulfilling her parents' dream. She was not resentful that money had been taken away from her, their heir. Because her parents had discussed the matter with her prior to their deaths, she was aware of their intent and fully supportive of their understanding of Christian stewardship.

The value the couple placed on higher education and their dedication to being good, disciplined stewards of God's provisions is perpetuated through the endowment. Each recipient is taught about both of these values, for they endure well beyond the lifetimes of the donors.

A well-to-do gentleman in a sizeable suburban church had given generously to the church throughout his lifetime. Partly because of his appreciation of well-maintained facilities, and partly from his desire to financially assist his first wife in her later years, he established a charitable remainder annuity trust that would support her for the rest of her life, and then benefit the church.

In his will, he established a testamentary charitable remainder annuity trust. The two trusts were to remain in existence until the death of his first wife, at which time they would be terminated. An endowed fund in an amount equal to the trusts' original amounts was to be established for his beloved church for the purposes of debt retirement and building maintenance. Excess in either trust above the original amount was to establish another endowed fund, with distributions to support two other denominational ministries in the community.

With the first distributions from the two new endowments, the congregation initiated the repair of several major facility needs, as well as a capital stewardship program to engage the entire congregation in upgrading the facilities across a three-year period. When the capital projects and plans were approved by the governing board, the gentleman's widow, who remained very active in the congregation and who had been the beneficiary of the gentlemen's other assets through his estate plan, commented that nothing would have pleased him more!

Clearly, this was a wise businessman and a good steward of the assets he had accumulated from his successful companies. He loved his family, his church, and his community. Had the plans not been well defined through the trusts and other documents, chaos and legal difficulties could have arisen. Not so in this case. His generosity will strengthen the congregation's ministries and the outreach of two community agencies for years and even generations beyond his lifetime.

While the concept of estate planning is a relatively new idea, the principles of managing the assets that God provides to us are biblical. Although it is not biblical in statement, the following comment, attributed to Andrew Carnegie, is certainly congruent with these principles: The man who dies rich dies disgraced.

It is not that biblical principles decry wealth. Rather, it is when accumulating or protecting wealth becomes the objective of one's life that the biblical principles insist on a shift to faithful obedience to our God as the One God. The same could be said for holding wealth without plans to use the resources that God has provided for the well-being of all concerned, particularly because one no longer needs the resources after death.

The magnificent biblical gift of generosity has crossed the generations from biblical times to our time. Giving and receiving are basic to our livelihood, whether they are done individually, with family, or with our congregation. We can learn from those who have shown us, through their planning and generosity, how the work of Jesus Christ can be enhanced and perpetuated by creative giving. Where individuals, families, and congregations stumble is in inadequate planning.

The one positive element that is consistent throughout the stories shared in this chapter is the essential role of effective planning. In the multitude of other stories that could have been told, the thread of planning would still have been consistently and necessarily present.

CHAPTER 19

A Financial Master Plan

Most businesses in North America have business plans that chart their futures. Goals are established, and evaluative criteria are defined. A business plan is often established for periods of one, three, and five years. The marketing strategy is a proactive part of the plan and certainly a part of the evaluative criteria. When marketing does not yield necessary business, the business plan is adjusted, or the business ultimately fails.

While the analogy of a business plan is not perfect for understanding the church, the reality is that one of the church's primary missions is to develop a marketing objective. Saving souls and making disciples are not passive activities; however, it is not unusual for a church to set an annual budget for expenditures with little regard to income.

One church had recently lost a large number of families to a new church. These families' contributions had represented over 25 percent of the previous year's income.

The finance committee established a budget that represented an increase of more than 10 percent over the previous year. The committee's approach to the need for significant increased revenue was to conduct a low-key campaign.

Several months into its disastrous year, the finance committee was certain of only one thing—it did not want to seek help from an outside consultant or to talk about money in the church. This is nuts!

Inevitably, the lack of financial planning causes increased challenges in the church. The finance committee often focuses on a survival view of cutting enough expenses to match income, with little regard for mission. New ministries and proper funding for growing them are negligible. The idea of addressing planned giving has little energy. Needed capital efforts are delayed, while the costs of projects continue to grow.

A negative culture develops about money. In this culture, the immediate need becomes the standard for communication, the theological issue of stewardship is seldom addressed, and the vision of the church suffers. Behind this is the theology of scarcity mentioned before.

While the issues of annual and capital campaigns have been discussed in previous books, the integration of all three streams of income into one plan has not been presented. A church's financial master plan involves intentional planning for annual, capital, and creative giving by a multifaceted financial leadership team. The question is not whether this approach can succeed; it is whether a particular community of faith has the will to implement it. Several hurdles must be crossed.

Financial leaders must be open to making a real change in the way they consider faith and money issues. The idea that a church can continue to do what it has been doing and expect different results based on increased sincerity or the careful wording in a brochure is just folly.

There must also be a radical shift in church leaders' attitudes away from the perception of limitation due to marginal resources. It is ironic that during the greatest explosion of discretionary income in the history of America, less money was saved, and the percentage of money given declined. Thus, the phrase "I would give more if I had more" is statistically untrue. With mainline churches experiencing a giving rate of around 2.5 percent of adjusted gross income, there is no statistical basis for this attitude of scarcity.

Recently while participating in some workshops, several participants were very sincere in expressing their belief that they were unique in having limited available resources. In one instance, the person was from a state identified as thirteenth in affluence and forty-seventh in generosity. In another case, a person suggested that her state was poor compared to mine, and that skewed my perspective. Yet my state is generally recognized as forty-ninth or fiftieth in personal income/personal wealth in comparative financial reports.

It is also common to hear a similar response from local church leaders who say something like, "You don't understand our church; our people have very little money available." This usually reflects an attitude conditioned by years of poor communication and persistent attempts to address money from the church's need.

Another hurdle to get past is the idea that focusing on one income source takes away from others. In other words, if we talk too much about the church's budget and regular giving, capital campaign giving will be hurt. Or addressing planned giving will hurt regular and capital giving. The financial leaders' fear is that basic giving to underwrite the church budget will be damaged. Based on our experience, however, a capital campaign most often enhances regular giving, as does planned giving, and this has been borne out by the research identified in a previous chapter.

The hurdle of too much financial communication also requires some intentional planning. A few years ago, during a consultation with a church facing serious financial challenges, the leaders were not very open to thinking differently or communicating more effectively. They wanted a magic bullet that would yield results without taking any steps of faith. Their solution was for the lender to forgive their massive debt or for a wealthy member to give an extraordinary gift to bail them out.

They said that when they had attempted to talk about money, families left the church and joined a well-known, growing church nearby. The irony was that the other church had a very aggressive annual campaign, a highly visible and successful planned giving program, and continual capital campaigns for several years to address their needs during their time of great growth. The other church addressed faith and money issues in the context of ministry and mission, not by whining about the church's financial needs.

Some churches have begun to look beyond the immediate shortfalls of a particular period by developing a broader ownership of faith and money issues, including different leadership structures and multifaceted approaches. Rather than maintaining a finance committee of a few people whose express purpose is to limit spending, a stewardship committee becomes the focus.

The stewardship committee frames the annual campaign, designs stewardship education approaches for all ages, develops the financial reports as an extension of the education efforts, and collaborates with the other financial groups. A different committee is responsible for the planned giving program, including policies, education, and materials. The finance committee collaborates with other groups in financial management, commercial financial relationships, and analyzing financial data. Others develop gift-acceptance policies, facility maintenance issues, and legal issues.

Then when the church needs to address capital needs, a group is developed for that specific project. This group might include a study committee, a building committee, and a capital campaign steering committee. All communication for all of these various financial leadership groups goes through the stewardship committee. Whereas the finance committee has most often had members like business owners, accountants, and bankers, the stewardship committee has educators, communicators, and sales-oriented members.

While this model has been implemented in a number of congregations, one common observation can be made. The structure can be developed without too much difficulty. The chairs of the various financial leadership groups can form a financial council for general oversight; however, one person must be the catalyst for the groups to function and communicate effectively.

Although some people might suggest that this should be the pastor, clergy do not seem to have the gift, training, or available time for this function, given their other responsibilities. The pastor must be supportive in terms of preaching, communicating, and personal priority. Pastors have seldom served well as catalysts.

In some instances, the business manager or financial secretary has served as the catalyst, but some people in these jobs do not have the leadership skills to coordinate other leaders. Other staff members have also had this responsibility, and this arrangement can work if they have the necessary gifts and the pastor's unwavering public support. Volunteer financial leaders with the necessary skills and leadership focus have also served as catalysts for designing and implementing a financial master plan for a church.

Developing a financial master plan does not diminish the issues of faith and spiritual value. Counting the cost is a basic tenet of discipleship and any meaningful commitment. It is hard to be a disciple or make a commitment if expectations are not understood. For the church to grow in spite of the financial challenges of this century, a more intentional and comprehensive approach that uses a financial master plan can provide desperately needed direction, broaden the ownership of financial issues, and make better use of members' varied gifts. With a financial master plan, communication can be improved, and revenue can be enhanced. An intentional plan that connects faith and money is one of the ways we can develop disciples.

CHAPTER 20

A Call to Action

During this time of unprecedented wealth in the United States, our silence about issues of faith and money has been deafening. What irony! A classic tenet of Christian theology is the continuing revelation of God in all creation. Living in an economic culture where the political landscape is defined by economic considerations ("It's the economy, stupid!"), we seem to have adopted a passive, whiny tone on the subject.

When the gap between the haves and have-nots is ever widening, when personal consumer debt is at the highest level in history, how can the church be silent on the connection between faith and money? The only exception to this is the televangelists' strange theology of prosperity that suggests that God intends for everyone to be rich. Although this view is an aberration, it seems to have worked well for the televangelists.

In this series of books, we have attempted to communicate a better understanding of the three basic tenets of faith and money that deal with annual giving, capital giving, and planned giving. But there are some common observations that merit consideration.

The first is theological. The issue of our relationship to money and possessions is one of the primary subjects in the Bible. There is no biblical silence on the subject of financial priorities. There is, however, a negative momentum that suggests that, despite what anyone might say, this subject should be considered separately from faith.

Actually, this is a variation of the ancient heresy of Gnosticism that suggests that material things have no spiritual value, so money cannot be connected to faith issues. Scripture would logically counter this notion.

Another negative view is that money is scarce. Outgrowths of the Depression, we often hear the excuses "our people are giving what they can," and "our people just don't have any money." With average giving calculated at around 2 to 3 percent or less, depending on who is calculating, the issue is whether God really owns it or not.

The theology of scarcity can consistently do more to negate positive growth and vision for a community of faith than most other issues. Money is a common denominator; it is required to fund programs and opportunities. Whenever there is a fundamental disconnect between faith and money, there is a lack of wholeness in understanding discipleship. How can a church create a budget—a major portion of which constitutes a fixed expense—without knowing how to promote increased income? More seriously, how does a community of faith try to develop and mature disciples without considering money, which is the common denominator of life in our culture?

The problem of creative giving is that we have not done a good job in the more basic areas of annual and capital giving, nor have we framed the connection between faith and money as the spiritual issue that it is. This requires an intentional strategy, energy, and critical thinking.

This applies to evangelism as well. An intentional approach would take a step back from the survivalist attitude of the institution's need and look at connecting faith and money as a critical part of the spiritual pilgrimage.

Think about it for a moment. If a family is committed to a mortgage, car payments, private schools, club memberships, expensive toys, and recreational shopping—along with the accompanying debt—then isn't this family's life defined by consumption instead of stewardship? And what are the adverse dynamics affecting a family in this condition? Is discipleship something to be fit in among other pastimes?

Our consumptive culture complicates the issue of faith and money on another level. When the church makes an annual appeal for financial support, it is often seen as focusing on the church's need for funding. In many settings, it is a seasonal event related to the time of year or the severity of the financial shortfall. And once the results are reviewed, we realize that we have not done all that well.

When the church wants to build or to retire debt, it often finds that less than half of its membership participates. And after addressing these two needs, there is often very little energy or leadership left to take on additional creative giving efforts.

Then there is the other experience that we have seen in recent years: the conversation with some who have been exposed to the idea of creative giving but have a difficult time making decisions. Annual and capital giving campaigns expect a response by a designated time, but planned giving is more open-ended. The deadline is before you're dead, and we tend to not think about ever actually dying.

In one conversation, an affluent professional couple in their fifties with significant real estate holdings and investments said that they were confused about making a planned gift. Would their wishes be carried out after they were gone? Who could be trusted? How do you craft such a plan? How relevant would their wishes be in ten, twenty, or fifty years?

With no children, they had great potential, but they had lived a life of self-indulgence. They gave to their church's annual efforts, and if their church had ever run a real capital campaign, then they could have made a six-figure gift if they had chosen to do so. But the matter of an irrevocable planned gift was just beyond their imagination.

They were also concerned about how planned gifts actually work. Yet when their church offered planned giving seminars to share this information, they could not find the time to participate.

In another case, a couple in their mid-seventies faced the twilight of their lives with health limitations. They owned several properties, including rental and lake real estate. They received several sources of retirement income, and they had no real financial limitations. They had also experienced significant exposure to the ideas and methods of planned giving. They had even explained the concept to friends, and they had helped solicit gifts from others, but they had never made such a gift. When asked why, both this couple and the one above said that the timing just wasn't right for them to make a decision.

So how do we move forward?

We believe that the church culture needs to change so that the connection between faith and money is a common consideration, instead of a seasonal event. Leadership can include the professional church staff, but it must also include key lay leaders who do not perceive themselves as fundraisers, but as disciple-makers.

There must be regular conversations, lessons, workshops, mailings, and, most of all, the expectation that our financial expressions reflect our discipleship experiences. The year-round and multi-year approaches we recommend are not gimmicks to wear people down by repetition, but rather recommendations of intentional strategies to keep this subject visible in the church landscape.

The call to action begins with you. Besides defining an ongoing financial expression of your faith, and in addition to regular giving and prayerful consideration of capital campaign support, you need to consider your own creative giving efforts. When you find obstacles to creative giving, make them a matter of personal prayer.

What would hinder you from acknowledging God's ownership of all that you have and your management of it? It is a lot easier to speak confidently about creative giving with others if you have considered it yourself. To talk about planned gifts with others while failing to make one yourself lacks integrity.

There is no shortage of financial resources available to the church and for God's purposes, but there is a shortage of positive, expectant leadership in making a clear connection between faith and money. But without making this connection, how real can your discipleship be?

We have often been asked to consult with churches, church agencies, and, occasionally, other nonprofit groups. Most can define their missions in some form, many can share their visions, and almost all agree that they have substantial financial needs. But we have been consistently dismayed at the leaders who believe that funding will somehow come from an undefined source without their having to communicate the need and, certainly, without their significant personal financial support.

We believe that the future of the church depends on how well we address issues of faith and money as primary considerations of our discipleship. It is as simple as the words of Christ found in Matthew 6:21 and 24:

For where your treasure is, there will your heart be also.

No one can serve two masters; for a slave will either hate the one and love the other, or be devoted to the one and despise the other. You cannot serve God and wealth.